THE DREAMER AND THE DREAM

Titles From GICPress

ORGANIZATIONAL CONSULTING: A GESTALT APPROACH
Edwin C. Nevis

GESTALT RECONSIDERED: A NEW APPROACH TO CONTACT AND RESISTANCE
Gordon Wheeler

THE NEUROTIC BEHAVIOR OF ORGANIZATIONS
Uri Merry and George I. Brown

GESTALT THERAPY: PERSPECTIVES AND APPLICATIONS
Edwin C. Nevis

THE COLLECTIVE SILENCE: GERMAN IDENTITY AND THE LEGACY OF SHAME
Barbara Heimannsberg and Christopher J. Schmidt

COMMUNITY AND CONFLUENCE: UNDOING THE CLINCH OF OPPRESSION
Philip Lichtenberg

BECOMING A STEPFAMILY
Patricia Papernow

ON INTIMATE GROUND: A GESTALT APPROACH TO WORKING WITH COUPLES
Gordon Wheeler and Stephanie Backman

BODY PROCESS: WORKING WITH THE BODY IN PSYCHOTHERAPY
James I. Kepner

HERE, NOW, NEXT: PAUL GOODMAN AND THE ORIGINS OF GESTALT THERAPY
Taylor Stoehr

CRAZY HOPE & FINITE EXPERIENCE
Paul Goodman and Taylor Stoehr

IN SEARCH OF GOOD FORM: GESTALT THERAPY WITH COUPLES AND FAMILIES
Joseph C. Zinker

THE VOICE OF SHAME: SILENCE AND CONNECTION IN PSYCHOTHERAPY
Robert G. Lee and Gordon Wheeler

HEALING TASKS: PSYCHOTHERAPY WITH ADULT SURIVIVORS OF CHILDHOOD ABUSE
James I. Kepner

ADOLESCENCE: PSYCHOTHERAPY AND THE EMERGENT SELF
Mark McConville

GETTING BEYOND SOBRIETY: CLINICAL APPROACHES TO LONG-TERM RECOVERY
Michael Craig Clemmens

INTENTIONAL REVOLUTIONS: A SEVEN-POINT STRATEGY FOR TRANSFORMING ORGANIZATIONS
Edwin C. Nevis, Joan Lancourt and Helen G. Vassallo

IN SEARCH OF SELF: BEYOND INDIVIDUALISM IN WORKING WITH PEOPLE
Gordon Wheeler

THE HEART OF DEVELOPMENT: GESTALT APPROACHES TO WORKING WITH CHILDREN, ADOLESCENTS, AND THEIR WORLDS (2 Volumes)
Mark McConville and Gordon Wheeler

BACK TO THE BEANSTALK: ENCHANTMENT & REALITY FOR COUPLES
Judith R. Brown

THE DREAMER AND THE DREAM: ESSAYS AND REFLECTIONS ON GESTALT THERAPY
Rainette Eden Fantz and Arthur Roberts

GESTALT THERAPY—A NEW PARADIGM: ESSAYS IN GESTALT THEORY AND METHOD
Sylvia Fleming Crocker

THE UNFOLDING SELF
Jean-Marie Robine

THE DREAMER AND THE DREAM

Essays and Reflections on Gestalt Therapy

Rainette Eden Fantz

Edited and with an Introduction by

Arthur Roberts

Preface by Gordon Wheeler and Epilogue by Dorothy Siminovitch

The Gestalt Institute of Cleveland Press

Chapter 1, "Metaphor and Fantasy" first appeared in: Fantz. (1983). "The use of metaphor and fantasy as an additional exploration of awareness." *The Gestalt Journal*, VI:2, 1983.

Chapter 2, "The Gestalt Approach To Dreams" first appeared as "Gestalt Approach" in: Fosshage & Loew. (1987). *Dream Interpretation*. New York: PMA Publishing.

Chapter 4, "Fragments of Gestalt Theory" first appeared in: Stephenson. (1978) *Gestalt Therapy Primer*. New York: Jason Aronson.

Fosshage & Loew. (1987). *Dream Interpretation*, is available from PMA Publishing, (714)-443-1744, Fax (714) 443-1745 or e-mail Ancharoff @ earthlink. net Costa Mesa. CA.

Gestalt Institute of Cleveland: 1517 Hazel Drive,
Cleveland, OH, 44106

Distributed by Routledge, Taylor & Francis Group
711 Third Avenue, New York, NY 10017
2 Park Square, Milton Park, Abingdon, Oxon OX14 4RN

ISBN 0-88163-299-6

Cover Design by Karen Pfautz
Cover photo of Rainette Fantz circa 1950 courtesy Lorian Fantz

For Karen

Le coeur a ses raisons…

ACKNOWLEDGMENTS

Many an acknowledgments page seems to begin with some statement about how this particular book "owes its existence to a great many people..." I doubted the truth of that judgment until I tried my own hand at putting a book together.

The first person to whom this book owes its existence is Gordon Wheeler. It was he who preserved Rennie's notes and papers (many of them hand-written), he who came up with the idea to turn them into a book, and he who entrusted the project to me. I thank him not only for this opportunity, but also for his warm friendship, remarkable generosity and grand intellectual repartee—all of which have in different ways affected my own work. He's been a model of committed concern, active engagement, and the living of the courageous life.

Several others who've been important to me need to be mentioned here. Alan Brody, Associate Provost for the Arts at the Massachusetts Institute of Technology, and Janet Sonenberg, professor of Theater Arts at M.I.T., have showered me with love and support from the start; I am deeply grateful to them both. Marc Singer, founder and CEO of ToggleThis Entertainment, has given me eleven years of friendship and, occasionally, privileged entrée into a penetrating and deliciously different mind. Lee Geltman, Kathy Hearn, Alan Robinson and my training group at the Gestalt Institute of New England have been an important source of community, inspiration and encouragement. Jill Ritchie, Lisa Shea and the rest of the staff at the Berklee College of Music Counseling Center provided the kind of warmth and support that every young therapist should be lucky enough to experience. Bob Lee, Ron Goldman, Allan Singer, Taylor Stoehr, and Deb Ullman have all been of considerable help in hashing out ideas related to this book. Rachel Barber of Harvard University helped me transcribe Dr. Fantz's notes and lectures, and Dorothy

Siminovitch, Rennie's student and friend, graciously contributed the final chapter of this book. My sincere thanks to them both.

I'd like to mention my parents as well: my father, who teaches me more and more every day; and my mother, whose courage and strength is exceeded only by her capacity to love and nurture. She's been an inspiration to me, and to many others.

And finally, I must mention the overwhelming support and encouragement of my companion, Karen Pfautz. Her kindness and intelligence have filled my heart and fired my imagination. She's my home, hearth, and family, and makes possible everything I do.

"Who is the potter, pray, and who the pot?"
—The Rubáiyát

CONTENTS

MAGIC AND METHODOLOGY: REFLECTIONS OF RENNIE

Teaching, like psychotherapy, is among the most existential of all the arts. It takes place, as Arch Roberts points out in his introduction to this collection, in the "space between," that living "place" or field which is both found and created, in the engagement of a person with *something to tell,* and an active listener, a person who brings his or her forming self to the encounter, in a state of readiness or availability to influence. Real teaching and learning, that is, transformative teaching—which is more than the mere rote absorption of "information" divorced from context and meaning—takes place and has to take place in relationship. The space of that relationship is ritual space, meaning the space created by a special, joined intentionality of two or more people, who come together out of a shared desire to participate in something new.

Of course, in the real world teachers do not always know how to offer this space, or offer themselves to it and in it; nor do students necessarily arrive at the door with the attitude and availability to risk this kind of contact. This was Rennie Fantz's special genius: to evoke, with a slight toss of the chin and a small sweep of one hand, a kind of magic circle, where new things might be felt and thought and dared—and then somehow to make that created space seem so inviting, almost intoxicating at times, and at the same time so *safe,* that you the student stepped willingly into the circle, and then found yourself saying, doing,

1

and feeling things you never thought you could (or would) do and feel—in some cases because you wouldn't have known, in words at any rate, that those thoughts and feelings and actions were even *there*. I remember Roger, a fellow student in a training program at a process group session, going after another student for some offense or habit, growing as I recall out of the fact that we all lived in a dorm together, under semi-communal conditions. Roger was reluctant to show, even perhaps to know just how tight and judgmental he felt, not only then but much of the time. Under a veneer of easy manners he kept up a steady beat of private judgments, of himself as well as others, which kept a safe gulf between him and other people. Everybody liked Roger; nobody felt he/she really knew him. As if in a trance, yet clear-eyed and alert in a new way, he followed Rennie into these "unattractive" feelings. Did he feel hard, cold?—*good*, Rennie thrilled to the chill of his steeliness, and Roger became interested in himself in a new way. Superior?—*exciting*, Rennie seemed to purr: go on, soar like an eagle above these tiny people, look down on them from a height they've never known, what a flight (but soon Roger felt lonely, and one by one he invited the rest of us to come on up and soar too, till finally the room was a wild dance of swoops and whoops and plunges, everybody tasting the eagle's life, and Rennie right there with us, somehow dancing and swaying, on painful feet that ordinarily took a full five minutes just to arrive at the second floor of the building. Controlling? —what *energy*, Rennie almost growled. Be the dictator of the world, order your minions, don't fight it, celebrate it, exult in it, and then *see where it takes you*. That new place, Rennie seemed to promise, will be new life, new freedom for the self—and perhaps contrary to our expectations and fears, a new kind of connection with others.

Where it took Roger was into sobbing, then laughing, finally resting—in the arms of the same person he had begun by attacking and pushing away. Stepping back out of the trance at last, a little blinking and bewildered, he began looking about to collect these strange new pieces of the self. "But if I—if I..." he

2

stammered, and then finally got it out: "if I just go around feeling whatever I really feel, being whatever I really am, then I can't help thinking I might just end up falling in love with people *all the time.*" His distress was so heartfelt and at the same time so innocent that it was almost comic; and yet nobody laughed—yet.

A sustained pause, while his words and his fear just hung there in the air—perhaps because they were shared by all of us, in one way or another. Rennie just looked at him, with a wistful sort of look, the tender wistfulness of a deep, deep compassion. And yet the eyes danced with devilment. "*My*—" she finally began, in a throaty stage whisper that somehow held and gently mocked the fear at the same time. That one word hovered, the space of a long breath, or one of those held silences in the theater. And then she finally finished, with a little throwaway toss of one hand: "my, *wouldn't that be—dire.*" Everybody held their breath while the suppressed giggle passed from her eyes to his belly, and then up to his shoulders, which began to quiver. And then everybody cracked up.

I can see those gestures, and those hands, through the mist in front of my eyes as I write this. Cruelly deformed, near useless hands, shriveled and twisted by thirty years of inflammatory arthritis, which slowly robbed her of everything—except everything that matters. In her last years, she could still lift a pencil, or a fork, once it was wedged between the frozen fingers— but she couldn't release it again, which she found "maddening"—a word she drew out with relish, as if to get the most out of this new feeling. She relished too the story told by the film director Jean Renoir, of his father the painter, who suffered from the same pitiless disease (in later years his paintbrushes had to be taped to his hands, and the tape would sometimes pull the skin away afterwards—and still he continued to produce monumental canvases of luminous joy and sensuality). "Master," exclaimed a boorish visitor at the dinner table, watching the artist's struggle just to eat, "but how do you ever *paint?*" "With my *dick,*" the normally prudish and mild-spoken Renoir shot back. "*Exactly,*"

Rennie threw back her head and chuckled out loud when I read her this passage, "— exactly. *Mutatis mutandis*, of course," she added, which is Latin for something like the same principle in a different situation. And then with great mock-solemnity: "You know I never agreed with Freud about *penis envy!*"

Why would she? Rennie reveled in charm, flirting, seduction, and being the center of attention, a star. But—and this was the secret of her magic, it seems to me—*she wanted everybody else to have these things too.* She saw the lover, the seducer, the flirt and the star in everyone she worked with, old or young, female or male, straight or gay or in between; and she drew on unseen, unimaginable resources of energy, will, and sheer courage, however much it took, until they and she found all these things and brought them out. This courage was of the essence in her work, and in the effect she had on others. We speak of embodiment in psychotherapy, and especially in Gestalt therapy— of the therapist's need to live what he/she teaches. How could you hesitate to dance down some uncharted path with Rennie as your guide, when the gallantry of her just walking in the room could take your breath away? Not that she ever called attention to her disability—on the contrary, she made you forget it, by inhabiting it so completely that she forgot it herself, preferring to lose and find herself again in the relationship, the work, the play, the new energy created in that space between. Yes, her hands were piteously, horribly deformed; but when she gestured (and she gestured constantly, "talking with her hands," as she said), what you saw was the gesture, not the disease. When she touched your arm or the back of your neck, what you felt was the touch, not the stiff and almost skeletal fingers. When she danced—and she did dance, on occasion, almost to the end,—what you saw was the dance, not the limitations. True, she danced in an ever-smaller circle, physically. But that circle grew larger, not smaller, as time went by, with growing room in it for all the possibilities of the ever-expanding self, and all the selves that couldn't resist that siren call, to step into the dance with her, and then take a part of it away with them when they left, somehow larger, more alive, more *encouraged*, in the root sense of the word, than when they came.

Great artists growing older—Renoir comes to mind again, or two more of Rennie's diverse favorites, Cervantes and Hokusai—grow through technique and pass beyond it, leaving method and movements and theories behind. Or rather, they transcend technique, so that method and magic become one. Rennie spoke of herself as following Perls in her work with dreams, metaphors, and fantasies, but actually she was on a course of her own, grounded to be sure in the work of her teachers, Perls and Goodman, From and others, but going well beyond some parts of that work in the direction of new energy, relationship, and wholeness. As she worked, supporting the client to act out a "projected part of the self" or articulate a "two-chair dialogue," the stakes were never just a matter of going back, to "unfinished business," "introjected shoulds," "repressed" desires and the like. All this was the past, the world of "explanations," which to her meant looking backwards. In Rennie's capable, disfigured hands the work was always forwards, always towards self-expansion and new life. The image or character of the dream was not just some old or forbidden self-element: it was a whole new land to explore, a new atmosphere to breathe or soar or plunge in, a new role to embody, as in the theater, which was her first professional training, and her career until illness cut it short in her thirties (it was in Thornton Wilder's "The Skin of our Teeth," she told me nearly forty years later, playing the lead role of the maid, going down on her knees and wondering every night if she could get up again, that she realized she needed a new line of work). The dream, the role, the metaphor or the person who draws your attention when you look around the room—for Rennie each of these held a message, and that message, if embraced, took you always in the direction of self-expansion and more life.

This background and this orientation led her to leaps and creative flourishes in teaching and therapy that likely would not have occurred to her own teachers and mentors. With a client battling lifelong depression, terrified of passing her mood-space on to a small sunny-faced daughter who still knew how to play, Rennie listened awhile to the long obsessive litany of phobias and fears, and then said, "Now be your *daughter*. Right here. Get down on the floor and be your daughter, and tell us what you *see*." Listening from the sidelines, I had forgotten the daughter by this time, my own attention caught by all the problems and the suffering. Rennie remembered, and went for the spot of life and color, out of a whole canvas painted with real and imagined darkness. In my own case, after listening to a dream where I kept going down to the cellar and finding cadavers in open coffins, she cut through a thicket of possible interpretations, role plays, and psychodramas with the question, "So what's dead in your life, and still unburied?" Nothing a client could bring, real or fantasized, shocked Rennie, no desire repulsed, no menacing darkness frightened her;—why should it, she lived with darkness encroaching every night, gaining a precious lost bit each new morning. "I suppose I'm dying by inches," Rennie would announce, as if above all she found this condition *interesting*— "but who isn't? I don't dwell on it. I think about what I can *do* today, what's new and around the corner."

In the darkness of the client's tragedy, the patient's depression and guilt, the student's heartbreak or anxiety and self-defeat, she always reached in and went for the light. Not in a pollyannish way, not to run from sorrow, loss and despair—but because "*who has the time?*" Don't avoid it, she seemed to say, reach for it, throw yourself into it, wallow in it if you like—and then *come out the other side*, and *live more intensely for it*. Yes, Rennie joined in pioneering a field, cocreating a method, cofounding and shaping an institute where some thousands of Gestalt practitioners have studied and trained over the past forty years (and a significant number of them have gone on to create other institutes, teaching and writing and training thousands more). These things are important; and at the same time to me, as to so many others of her students and colleagues, her influence was more specific, in my own life and work. Faced with a problem, a crisis, an impasse with a client or a friend, I imagine her voice, saying something like, "go ahead, *see* them, *be* with them, let them know you're really there, you're not afraid of all that darkness—but *don't stop there*, don't live there. That's what they're already know how to do. Go with them to a new place. In every picture, every dream, every tragedy your client brings you, there's something alive, some new energy. Go with that, and you'll help them create something new." Steeped in the artistic history and cultural legacy of the Western tradition, Rennie saved her best reserves of energy for the new thing, and that new thing nourished her, restored her, and then nourished others who experienced her, experiencing themselves with her in some new way.

To Rennie this was Gestalt: the idea that we can choose what we attend to, and that *there where we invest our attention, we invest ourselves*, enacting and then becoming that attentional object and process. "I guess I always choose the person who judges me, anyway who I think judges me," a student struggled to explain, "and then I try to please them, just like with my mother, and it doesn't work, and I don't even notice everybody else, and I feel worthless, and I —" and on and on, down one of those self-defeating spirals we all know in some form or other, where we somehow trigger one of those early trance states, sequences where the first step seems to contain the last in a kind of hopeless, seamless self-lock. *"Choose differently,"* was Rennie's simple response. "Right here, right now, look around the room, take your time, look at each person, and *choose differently*. And then see what happens." As I recall, the group never went back to the "issue" the person had started with, of trying to "work out her relationship" with another group member, someone she was experiencing as rejecting and judgmental. It just didn't seem the point. Rather, we all followed Rennie, as soon as she mentioned it, down the path of something new. As I remember it now, what followed was transformative, and for more than one person.

When I then asked Rennie, as her co-leader-in-training, how she built that intervention, she had to pause, and deconstruct what was second nature to her. "Well, I suppose it was that word *always,*" she mused out loud. "It stands out. Why would she *always* do the same thing, when life is so different, at every moment? And then those words *everybody else.* They're already there, you see, they have a place in the story, you don't have to make them up. They're there, but she's not attending to them. What if she did? That would contradict the always. You see, then it becomes interesting. *I follow my interest.* Hers is frozen, so I follow mine. Her attention is fixed, so I let mine play." This is teaching: the kind of inspired self-revelation that makes the complex simple, so the simple can become complex in a new way. It is also magic—magic and methodology, the one informing and the other enlivening, the two essential poles in the creation of anything new.

How do we then pass on that teaching, and even some of that magic, so that all of us who knew Rennie can have a new "hit" of her presence, her vision—and those who didn't can taste that unique flavor as well, and stand for a moment at that special point of view? Well, first of all by living it, Rennie would say. You can't pass on what you haven't got. A tradition, a methodology loses all its magic when we stop living it fresh, in the new situation we find ourselves in with every client, every student, at potentially every moment. We create our world and our selves in that world, actively and continuously: this is the very essence of the Gestalt constructivist model, and the Gestalt vision as Rennie lived and taught it. And then there are the stories, vignettes and memories that capture a gesture and a moment, in the enactment which is both the example and the thing itself. In the theater, actors speak of the "defining gesture," the look or pause or motion that embodies and renders the character for the audience. Rennie was mistress of these gestures, no doubt from her own grounding in theater, and when we share an anecdote it is to recapture the whole of the person, and the whole

8

of that vision, to make it our own and use it ourselves in some new way.

And then we have the writings. Rennie had many great loves: her daughter and grandchildren, first of all, her friends and colleagues, students and clients, art and music (the grand piano stood unused after her daughter, also a musician, grew up and left home), the spoken word—and the written word. She wrote flowingly and well, slowly and by hand necessarily, with few corrections, in a clear script that belied the frozen condition of her fingers. She was off-hand about her written work, published and unpublished; yet she did take the trouble to assemble it and give it to me before she died, an impressively large packet for a "non-writer." And impressively packed with the insights and perspective that she both drew from and gave to the Gestalt model, the "figures of attention," as she would say, that she selected and invested her own attentional energy in, to make something new. And all of it in her own inimitable voice, which is our common field from her unique point of view. Thanks to the gracious permission of Lori Fantz, and the editorial intelligence and dedication of Arch Roberts, that point of view is here in written form, for all of us to hear and interact with, and use for our own living and our own work. To me that voice comes off the page and inspires again. I hope and believe it will for you as well.

The last night of Rennie's life I sat with her in a hospital room in Cleveland. For the several days she had drifted in and out of consciousness, finally settling all that last day into a deepening coma. Her frail body—she can't have weighed 90 pounds at this point, barely displacing the covers she lay under—had ceased to take up and use the growing array of medicines that had both sustained her for so many years, and perhaps finally were killing her now; the decision had been reached to terminate active treatment, continuing only fluids intravenously. Her daughter Lori was exhausted from the long vigil, and went home for a night with her children. Toward evening, unexpectedly, Rennie rallied, regaining full alertness, alive again to the possibilities of one more evening with people she loved. We spoke of her daughter, her grandchildren, then of death and dying ("I'm tired," was all she said about it, then adding with a twinkle, "but you've got to admit, I've put it off for a long, long time!") But soon her attention swung to back to life. Now we spoke of theater, of what I'd seen in New York lately, of the new Fagles translation of the *Iliad* I'd sent her some months before ("virile," was her word for it, but she didn't finish it, because it had become too heavy for her to lift). I offered to sit with her through the night, which I had already promised Lori I would do, and the others left, Rennie's friend and colleague Dorothy Siminovitch the last to go. And then we spent the last night of Rennie's life together—singing show tunes. I don't remember now how we started talking about the legacy of the twentieth century American musical, equal in her mind to opera, which she treasured both for melodic beauty and for its lyric celebration of *intensity of feeling*—love, loss, hope and celebration. And then she began singing, first bits and pieces of old favorites and soon whole songs, in a voice that was weakened but still full of music, and I joined in. "There's no business like show business," she lilted out softly, and her head rocked back and forth on the pillow; then right into "Blue Moon," or "I'm just a girl who can't say no —" till we lost our way in the words ("But that wasn't me," Rennie added, speaking of herself now in the past tense, "I knew how to say yes, and I knew how to say no.") Some songs we sang whole, and some in snatches. "They say that falling in love is wonderful—" and "I'm gonna wash that man right outta my hair." I reminded her that the role of Sabrina she'd once played, from Skin of Our Teeth, had been played in the 50's by the musical star Mary Martin to Helen Hayes's Mrs. Antropus, live on Playhouse 90 when I was a small boy. Mary Martin had the best of it, she murmured—the maid has all the best lines. And that took her further into Rodgers and Hammerstein, and on back to Rodgers and Hart, "Bewitched bothered and bewildered," "My funny Valentine," or "If they asked me, I could write a book—" Sometime after midnight she said she was tired, and told me to go home and sleep. She was fine, she said, and would see me tomorrow. Next morning she was awake and alert again for a time, speaking with friends and family, then slipping by degrees back into unconsciousness. She died that evening, as her friends and colleagues at the Gestalt Institute of Cleveland, many of them former students, gathered for the annual faculty retreat dinner/dance. She passed over as we were dancing, leaving her depleted body in the bed, dancing with us again as her real self.

That was Rennie; in the words of her favorite poet of all, we shall not see the like of her again ("Ah, Shakespeare's women," Rennie exulted. "Lady MacBeth—now there's a role." "Did you ever play her?" I asked? "Oh yes," was the reply, "and I was *evil*. Did you know I could be evil?"). And yes, we did ask her, and she did write a book: this is it. She went out as she wanted to live, singing and dancing. As a legacy she left us the ripples of her spirit and the clarity of her words in these essays. And now?—these lines from her beloved Irish poet/dramatists come to mind:

> Once out of nature I shall never take
> My bodily form from any natural thing,
> But such a form as Grecian goldsmiths make
> Of hammered gold and gold enamelling
> To keep a drowsy Emperor awake;
> Or set upon a golden bough to sing
> To lords and ladies of Byzantium
> Of what is past or passing, or to come.

For us who are still in nature her message was and is the same: we too can sing.

Gordon Wheeler
Cambridge, Massachusetts
Spring, 1998

EDITOR'S NOTE

The essays and reflections in this volume are brimming with anecdotes from the clinical practice of the late Rainette Fantz. Before switching careers and becoming a founding member of the Gestalt Institute of Cleveland, Fantz spent many years as a professional actor—and in her remarkable therapeutic style we can see the influence of that earlier chapter in her life.

Her clinical work is polished with a poetic grace and aesthetic sensibility which never shies away from the truth of the interaction between herself and her clients (we see in this book that she's as comfortable telling us about her "failures" as her "successes"). Her keen sensitivity and openness to genuine engagement underlie an imagination which never ceased to see the *possibilities* inherent in the clinical situation—she had an almost unfailing intuition as to what-goes-with-what, where, and when. This intuition, as we'll see, was less of a mysterious "gift" or "talent" than it was the result of her dedication to her craft, and especially her willingness to be fully present in the moment with another person (a skill which is also the core of the actor's art).

Fantz's intimate involvement with the theatre is central to an understanding of her way of working. My pleasure in editing the essays which follow has been that they've inspired me to reflect on some of the questions about the relationship between theatre and therapy which have been preoccupying me for some time (as indeed they continue to do, for the relationship between the two fields is as bottomless as both). I also came to realize that because Fantz's essays are so deceptively simple and eminently enjoyable, it's easy to miss their profundity; it's easy to miss the deep well of experience and knowledge from which she continually draws inspiration. Yet there is a great deal we can

13

learn by looking further into this well, and specifically, further into the relationship between theatre and therapy, between actor and therapist.

A final word—or caveat: while few will agree with *all* of the sentiments Dr. Fantz expresses herein (I for one do not), there is something in her approach that appeals to clinicians of every stripe and theoretical persuasion. Although she is an "old school" Gestaltist—with a theoretical framework and language which are grounded in the Individualist tradition—she is clearly working against the limitations of a strictly Individualist model. Her clinical practice, while emerging from the language and foundation of Individualism, is thoroughly field-oriented; she manages to integrate the best of Gestalt insights and practice into a seamless therapeutic process.

With all the current talk of old *"versus"* new styles of Gestalt therapy, competing and even *"incompatible"* paradigms of thought, it's tempting to take up residence in one or another camp and then do our best to promote the truths of that side. But we sometimes need to remind ourselves (I sometimes need to remind myself) that "old" and "new," "Modern" and "Postmodern" are in the end nothing more, or less, than names. Ultimately, we all of us need to see through and beyond these conceptual dualities and begin the difficult, never-ending work of synthesizing the entire field—old *and* new, Modern *and* Postmodern. This is the very activity of living—the ongoing reorganization of the field, the ongoing creative adaptation to an ever-changing world. As a community struggling to support differences and celebrate commonalities, Fantz offers us a shining example. Here we have an account of someone who managed to arrive at her own synthesis while remaining open to the possibility—the necessity— of ongoing change.

Arthur Roberts
Boston, Massachusetts
Spring, 1998

THEATRE & THERAPY: A PROLOGUE

The heroic struggle of the actor
is to establish a relationship with the audience
an I THOU
filling in the space
finding the real
the real feeling between us
       —Julian Beck, co-founder of the Living Theatre

Tragedy is when we are ruined by our insufficiency,
comedy is when we can relish it.
       —Adam Phillips, *Terrors and Experts*

Therapy, in a very real sense, *is* theatre. It's a dramatic event in which story emerges from the interaction of embodied players, each affecting the other in a continuously unfolding dance. It's also a form of entertainment—and not only in the sense of the ancient admonition to healers that they "keep the patient entertained while nature works the cure." Both therapist and actor are entertainers if we understand that word in its original sense: *to entertain* comes from the Latin *inter tenere*—to hold between. Actor and the audience, therapist and client *hold something between* each other. This is the crux of theatre, and the critical ingredient of therapy; on every stage and in each consulting room, a space is created for the *story* which necessarily arises when two people come into contact with one another.

15

And in each of these creative pursuits, the art consists of precisely this: the way in which the story is wooed, and—once wooed—the way that it's held in the space between.

The skills required to be a good practitioner of these arts are not often taught in schools, and not easily acquired even when they are. The actor (or therapist) first learns to let herself *live*— fully, sensuously, courageously, consciously. This means nothing more or less than that she allows herself to be roundly affected by her world. Instead of turning away from the unformulated experience of her inner life, instead of fleeing from the hard impact of outer events, she opens herself to everything— especially other people. She becomes a willing conduit for the sometimes terrifyingly intense passions which exist within and without her, and cultivates the ability to give form and expression to what she finds in her soul. She becomes acquainted with her totality and—with whatever help she can find—develops the courage to explore regions of experience which others will not, so that she might bring new light to dark places. She acquires the patience to dwell in these places with her audience (or her client), for as long as the story demands. And finally, she develops skills such that—when necessary—she is able to guide herself and her companions *through* the darkness, to whatever daylight awaits on the other side.

It may at first be difficult to see the parallels between the actor's craft and the therapist's—between theatre *(theatron)* and therapy *(therapeia)*—but historically, etymologically and intuitively, the two are intertwined. We can begin to see into their complex relationship when we consider that the ritual event of theatre has been implicated in the process of healing since at least classical antiquity, when Aristotle wrote his celebrated treatise on communal catharsis and the nature of tragedy. The outward correspondence between the two fields has continued to the present day, and even a cursory survey shows that the common language which we've come to associate immediately with psychotherapy ("insight", "conflict", "catharsis") has its home in the language and theory of classical drama. What's more, many of the guiding metapsychological speculations which inform modern psychotherapeutic practice have been handed down to us from theatre. Freud anchored his revolutionary conception of human psychological development on the title character in Sophocles' great play, *Oedipus Rex*, and in doing so, he re-affirmed in our era the ancient affiliation between the two disciplines—and made plain the similarity between psychotherapeutic insight and that older form of psychological understanding, the theatre.

Not only psychoanalysis, but many other schools of thought in modern psychotherapy owe a debt to the world of the stage. Psychodrama and Transactional Analysis are centrally (though differently) concerned with role-playing, and Gestalt therapy in particular claims several influences from among our century's theatrical luminaries. Fritz Perls was inspired by Max Reinhardt of the *Grosses Schauspielhaus* in Berlin and the *Theater in dem Redoutensaal* in Salzburg, and Paul Goodman was influenced early on by theatrical sources ranging from Japanese Noh-theatre to Jean Cocteau (he later wrote plays for Julian Beck and Judith Malina of the Living Theater in New York, and had a powerful influence on their development in turn) (Stoehr, Taylor; personal communication).

The evolution of theatre and therapy in the 20th century has shown a remarkable parallelism, as each field exerted its profound (and reciprocal) influence on the other. Since the birth of psychology as a distinct discipline (roughly contemporary with the later decades of the 1800's), theatre artists around the world have drawn extensively upon the insights of modern psychological thought—even as psychologists such as Freud, Perls, Goodman, Moreno and others were drawing inspiration and ideas from the world of the stage to create the modern ritual of psychotherapy. Stanislavski's ideas at the Moscow Art Theatre were influenced by the great French psychophysiologist Theodule Ribot; Meyerhold's "biomechanics" were shaped by Pavlov's groundbreaking work in Russia; the deeply introspective American acting method of Lee Strasberg owed a tremendous debt to Freud and psychoanalysis; and Sanford Meisner's response to the overwhelming interiority of Strasberg's approach mirrored a parallel situation within psychotherapy: interpersonally-oriented therapists such as Harry Stack Sullivan, Karen Horney, Erich Fromm and others began to gain a wider audience at roughly the same time that Meisner was encouraging actors to get out of their heads and put their attention *outside*—on the other real, live actors—in order to find the reality of a given scene. (Sonenberg (with Roberts), in press).

But why this powerful correspondence? Why should such seemingly disparate fields show—upon closer inspection—such a pronounced affinity for one another? And—particularly important for the therapist—why does the event we know as theatre have such a powerful impact on the psychological imagination? Why have so many pioneers of modern psychotherapy claimed theatre as a seminal influence on their thought?

Taken together, theatre and psychotherapy form a fold of that continuum of human endeavor which seeks to explore our place in the universe—and they do so in highly ritualized fashion. The underlying structure of both is essentially the same: the participants—by virtue of a social arrangement—agree to meet at a predetermined time and place in order to tell emotionally charged stories about what it means to be human. These seemingly simple structural parameters account for the profound similarity of the two fields; they amount to the intentional evocation of a transformative ritual space.

It is this space that forms the cornerstone of both theatre and therapy, and the kinds of transformations which take place within it are responsible for the striking historical confluence of the two disciplines. Theatre is a communal event in which two parties (audience and actor) can experience a kind of salubrious emotional release through partaking in the live, immediate experience of an unfolding story. Similarly, modern psychotherapy is the ritual evocation of a transformational space in which a living story is enacted and experienced. *It was psychotherapy's intrinsic similarity to the ritual space of theatre* which Freud, Perls and others recognized. And it is this ritual setting which lies at the base of the two fields' familiarity.

*   *   *

Both theatre and therapy are fundamentally defiant acts. Each inevitably calls into question the ways in which we as a society have failed to live with ourselves, our world, our fellows. In the last century, the great movements in both fields have consistently been prompted by burning discontent, and championed by men and women who were convinced that there was a better way for people to exist together—a better way to struggle through the vicissitudes of life than by blindly adhering to deadening, antiquated rules of social conduct. Max Reinhardt wrote in 1929 that:

> "Our general social ideal is stoicism—always to be unmoved or at least to appear so. Passion, bursts of feeling and fancy, are ruled outside the bounds. In their place we have set up in a row common stereotyped forms of expression that are part of our social armor. This armor is so rigid and constricted that there is hardly any room for natural action... At weddings, christenings, burials, festivities we make out of hand-shaking and bowing, out of frowns and grins, a ghostly play, in which the absence of feeling is shocking." (Reinhardt, 1929).

Familiar ideas indeed for anyone drawn to Gestalt therapy.

But if theatre and therapy are both about telling a story—about creating a meaningful narrative—why is this seemingly simple endeavor so consistently linked to social turbulence? Why is telling a story so dangerous to the status quo? The answer is in part due to the fact that stories told in the theatre and in psychotherapy are enacted stories. The *telling* of stories within ritual space leads to the *enactment* of related stories, which may themselves be slightly different from the originals, and may themselves become subject to reflection. Live enactment is inherently unpredictable, and there is always the possibility that a new and slightly different (or markedly different) story will emerge. This unavoidable unpredictability of live storytelling is threatening to the pervasive hegemony of social rules and conditioning. Men and women are ever trying to live more comfortably, but authentic engagement in the service of a story demands that we truly see and hear an other—*all* of her—and such an encounter never makes the promise that it will be comfortable.

Social rules and regulations generally emerge with the best of intentions and later rigidify into oppressive codes of conduct which promote the very discomfort they originated to assuage. The pull towards social order and uniformity often only allows for the feeling (and recounting) of certain kinds of experiences; others are proscribed, actively discouraged and suppressed. There is an insidious correspondence between society's rules and the stories which we are allowed to tell about ourselves—and an even more troubling connection between what's acceptable to others "out there" and what becomes acceptable to us "in here." Because of this—and because good theatre and good therapy involve exposing those social customs which have become numbing and deadening—which have become *an*-aesthetic—there is a similarity between the results of each: good acting can wake us up, shock us into a recognition of our own existence, inflame our sense of injustice, and show us the actions which we make and at the same time attempt to disavow.

Good therapy also contains these moments of shocking recognition and insight; it can break our confluence with inhibiting social rules which no longer serve, and restore our sense of vitality, vigor and abundance. In each endeavor, we aim for *more life* in the face of the forces which constrain us: instead of turning away from our energies, we enter into them; instead of *reflexively inhibiting* our natural impulses, we *selectively inhabit* them.

But there is, inevitably, a danger in meeting life on its own terms—and this is in part the reason why theatre as a vocation and an institution has almost always existed on the periphery of respectable society. In authoritarian regimes, it is among the first art forms to be severely curtailed (or, if not done away with outright, entirely co-opted by the state), and its practitioners are among the least rewarded in a culture's fiscal economy. In part, the reason for these phenomena is due to the revolutionary power inherent in the enacting of a live story. Theatre is by definition a space in which the society at large *tells stories* about itself, to itself; it's purpose is "…to hold,/ as 'twere, the mirror up to nature; to show/ virtue her own feature, scorn her own image,/ and the very age and body of the time his form/ and pressure." The images we see in this mirror—the stories we're told—are often unpalatable; they show those aspects of ourselves which we'd rather not acknowledge, and which we usually push aside. Like Hamlet's roving band of players, the stories told in the theatre are stories without a home.

In a similar way, the stories told in psychotherapy are stories which have nowhere else to go. We are often the last resort for the person who is trying to make sense of his experience in the face of a world which seems to be ordering him not to feel what he feels. Our client comes to us in a state of distress because so much of his experience has been relegated to the periphery; in many cases, he's not only unable to formulate it in any kind of meaningful way, but he's also been made aware that he's not supposed to speak of it. Certain aspect of his experience have become both *inassimilable*—because of introjected cultural notions of right and wrong—and *inadmissible* in the social arena—because of the unwritten rules governing social discourse. When this happens, we find ourselves barred at both ends—effectively stripped of the ability to synthesize particular aspects of our experience and situate them within the ongoing narrative by which we understand the world; we can neither formulate our experience on our own nor share it with others.

In the course of therapy—just as in the course of a theatrical performance—the stories which cannot be understood in isolation nor told in the world are held between two parties in a protected space, temporarily safe from the need to comply with outer demands. In this space, over the course of their telling and enacting, the stories without a home—which seemed so perplexing and shameful to us at first—are seen to be stories of liberation. By the end, this sometimes troubling encounter with an other has somehow been fortifying, and we leave psychotherapy as we leave the theatre: transformed. We are moved to a place of solidarity with our selves and our world; we're brought to acknowledge our potentials and longings at the same time that we forgive ourselves for our frailties and imperfections.

*   *   *

Rainette Fantz was a professional actress before switching careers and becoming a founding member of the Gestalt Institute of Cleveland. Her second career was inevitably molded by her first, and the skill she brought to her work as a therapist had its roots firmly embedded in the soil of the theatre. In reading her lectures and clinical papers, we gain some insight into the way that an actor does what she does, and the way an inspired therapist makes continual use of her self in her work with clients of all kinds. In her writings, Fantz gives us entrée into the creative process of an individual whose imagination was striking in its inventiveness—and in the process we begin to realize that creativity is not only the result of being "gifted" or "talented" with imagination (though Fantz was both), but rather emerges from the therapist's willingness and ability to fully engage her clients, using *every* aspect of the material at hand to further the telling of the story which is unfolding between them.

Fantz learned this in the theatre. Like therapist and client, actors and audience embark upon a jointly agreed-upon venture: the audience pays the actors to tell them a story. To the untrained eye, this setup seems to be a one-way street: "Entertain us" the audience seems to be saying, "Tell us a story about ourselves, and we will go home happy." But this is only one perspective—the observer's. From the other side of the stage, any honest actor will tell you that the interaction between herself and her audience is nothing like a one-way street; the story which unfolds in the theatre on any given night (and the actor's performance as part of it) is inevitably molded by the engagement and response of the crowd (and here compare Fantz commenting on the clinical situation: "...your energy and that of your client must compliment and build upon one another in order for [experiments] to burgeon and worlds enlarge.") A particular theatrical performance is as much a product of the audience's participation as it is of the grueling work which the actors put into learning their craft and rehearsing their roles. The *meaning* of the story which is told always emerges from the interaction between *this* particular audience and *these* particular actors on *this* particular night. The interactive, dynamic nature of live theatre and live therapy constitutes their effectiveness, and ensures that any two performances will seem as different from one another as any two cases of depression.

It's also important to be aware of the distinct roles that each participant in such rituals must play. After all, actors and audience, therapist and client have decidedly different responsibilities: the audience comes to the actor's place of work, for example, and pays a fee. For her part, the actor is expected to lead the enterprise—to take action and deliver the goods. Things, of course, aren't so simple, because the audience doesn't merely sit passively taking in information—and at any rate, by coming to the theatre, *they* have actually taken the first step. Or was it the actors who made the first move, by choosing a play and rehearsing it? But didn't they choose a play in accordance with what they imagined the audience would pay to see?... Clearly, to attempt to trace the precise origin of the event called "theatre" is an exercise in futility; the best we can say is that *it happens*. All of the participants allow themselves to be swept up in the process even as each has his own ideas about his particular role and place within it.

An important implication of this fact, and the fact that the actor is paid to "tell a story," is that it establishes a structure which serves to organize the ensuing interaction. Because of the arrangement, he can't simply give free reign to every impulse he feels while working; he must stay within the bounds of the script so that the larger task at hand (the telling of the story) is accomplished. The story is the *raison d'etre* for the joint enterprise. This means that occasionally it's necessary for the actor to "...force his soul... to his own conceit." In other words, he must occasionally make creative use of his experience *in order to further the telling of the story*. He must *evoke* the story—summon it from its hiding place on the periphery into the space *between* himself and his audience. This requires that he occasionally subjugate certain impulses in deference to the larger task of the jointly agreed-upon venture—just as the therapist will not haphazardly make manifest every impulse or utter every thought which occurs to him while working with a client. This is another important sense in which the craft of the actor and the craft of the therapist are remarkably similar: each is engaged by someone else to use the self in service of agreed-upon work (and by "self," I here mean the actor's or therapist's entire *being*: physical body, voice, feelings, thoughts, intuitions, awareness, etc).

The therapist's self—and the actor's—we know in Gestalt terms to be the very *process* of creativity. "Self" is not an entity, it is experience being synthesized. In the situation of the theatre, we can see clearly that self is *not* the creative activity of some bounded organism roaming its environment, endlessly in search of objects to ingest or manipulate—this is one story *about* the self, but not the self *per se*. In the theatre (as well as in psychotherapy) we see especially clearly that the activity of the self is regulated by the story in which it is currently discovered. In other words, *the self organizes experience in accordance with the narrative in which it currently exists.* When we envision an isolated self searching the desert for water, we see a self which organizes experience according to the aesthetic demand of that particular situation. However, when we enter a different kind of situation—a situation like the theatre or like psychotherapy, for example—the self which appears is that synthetic unity which organizes experience according to an altogether different aesthetic demand. In the case of theatre and therapy, the demand is for *entertainment*—for a holding between; it results in a self which organizes experience in such a way that it tells itself about itself. The overarching story is a story in service of a story.

Another way of saying this is that the self is that instrument by which story tells itself, and by which story is told. When we "let ourselves go" (when we "let our selves go"), we enter into and become our immediate situation—our activity flows easily along the invisible lines of force which move the larger narrative along. And since a story needs at least two people in order to exist, the self is seen to be inseparable from the other; indeed it is seen as the instrument of *connection* with the other. To be creatively engaged as an actor or a therapist means that one opens oneself to the demands of the situation—one releases oneself into the contact. *Whatever* is being experienced in the present moment is accepted and synthesized; it is not avoided or turned away from because of a notion that it "doesn't fit" or "shouldn't be here." When practiced well, this kind of stance leads to profound openness, alert relaxation and a kind of playful poise. There is nothing to fear, because everything has its place. Fantz embodied these qualities in her work. She accepted the material at hand—whether it seemed agreeable or no—and let her work flow naturally from it; nothing was alien to her, nothing unnotable.

When some aspect of the emerging story seems to threaten the very structure which makes possible its continued telling, the therapist (or the actor) must make creative use of that experience, too. She must become a *bricoleur*. Instead of shying away from the present reality, instead of avoiding what's actual, the bricoleur works with it. She follows her experience as it's organized and synthesized in accordance with the aesthetic demand of the current situation. She trusts that this process itself is what sustains and furthers her connection to the other, and their shared world. For the bricoleur—be she actor or therapist—every event is of interest, every experience yields up its treasure which furthers the unfolding of the present. Feelings and thoughts which "don't fit"—which would seem to do damage to the integrity of the larger task—are accepted and transformed in the service of that task. This is the essential notion behind the consummately Gestalt idea of *using* our subjective experience as helpful information (in contrast to the idea of countertransference as something to be avoided in the treatment situation). It is also the essential notion behind the common admonition to the beginning actor to "*Use* it!"—to enlist whatever is current in his experience in the service of bringing life to his work on the stage.

*   *   *

The actor, by long detours, strict discipline and profound willingness, becomes an expert in interest. She trains in the art of making contact. Her interest in herself and her world is what allows her to explore those disturbing aspects of experience which are too terrifying, shameful or otherwise troubling to be brought to light. In service of her calling and her craft, she plunges herself willingly into the deepest recesses of her being—where our illusions about ourselves are necessarily shattered. In these dark places, we come face to face with what is most harrowing about the life we all share: our finitude, our smallness, our lies—but also, in these very same places, we discover our grandeur, our decency, and our love. In performance, the great actor will shake us to the core precisely because she's come into contact with these insurmountable realities; she's been confronted by her existence and *must* present it to the world. We're sometimes flustered by the disquieting impact which such a performer can have on us— we're simultaneously drawn in and disturbed; troubled and strangely thankful. We've witnessed ourselves in another, and we have been changed.

In this sense, the actor's craft is about saying the unsayable; it's about bringing deeply buried aspects of the self to the surface, and displaying them before a public gaze. And somehow, this process is healing—for actor and audience alike. The further one goes into studying the processes of theater or of therapy, the more difficult it is to distinguish between actor and audience or between therapist and client. To be sure, each has different roles to play, but the roles together form a meaningful whole; they implicate and constitute each other. When functioning well, theatre and therapy serve to bring self and other into a kind of communion in which their separateness is preserved: they are united in service of the story between them.

As therapists, it's important to note that when a good actor invites and evokes this communion, a he does not *tell* the audience what to feel, but rather *allows* the audience to feel what it will. The difference is tangible. Overblown performances in

27

which emotions are foisted upon an audience generally result in a collective cringe and a bad review—nobody likes to be told how to react. But we stand to gain from observing a skillful actor ply his craft. His dramatic expression is perfectly attuned to the receptivity of the audience (the other)—his feelings are genuine, his movements fitting; he is not posturing or showing off his skills. By the paradoxical road of strict discipline he has arrived at attuned spontaneity—spontaneity in service of the task at hand.

Fantz exhibited this characteristic as well. It can be seen not only in the way her clients respond to her interventions, but in the clinical flexibility she displays in her work. Here we see one of the hallmarks of mastery, shared by actor and therapist alike: thorough knowledge of a given craft combined with the unselfconscious creativity to work freely within its structure.

We often think of structure as something which limits freedom, but structure and freedom are inseparable. In theatre and therapy, we see clearly that structure is not the enemy of freedom but its necessary counterpart. For an actor, structure is given in part by the script and in part by the audience. The script only has meaning in relationship to the audience for which it is performed. The audience, in turn, gives life to the actors—without audience, there would be no actors, without actors, no audience. It is within this structure imposed upon the players by the script and the audience that there is the freedom to act—to *play* the play—and it is because of this structure that the actor's actions are infused with meaning. Once an actor has allowed the play to seep into her bones, to inhabit her soul, she has the freedom to *live*—vigorously—within the boundaries of that play. Any feelings that emerge, any impulses that arise, are grist for the mill—everything is directed toward the furthering of the unfolding story. Everything has a place.

The parallels to the therapist's craft are clear. The dramatic structure of therapy is what allows the therapist to live truthfully, resolutely, and in such a way that the emerging story is invited to be told. Both therapist and client come to the situation with all kinds of beliefs which help to organize the interaction: one person is coming to be helped, the other is there to help; one is going to pay, the other to be paid, etc. The resulting structure is the theatre in which therapist and client encounter one another, and again, it's *the structure that grants the freedom*. Working within it, both parties find the space to *play*. They are contained by the structure, supported by it, and free to improvise because of it.

Fantz shows this willingness to play. She's delightfully dauntless. One gets the sense that she could do absolutely anything with a client without in any way violating the aesthetic integrity of the situation. Her clinical behavior wasn't inhibited by abstract codes of conduct dictating what a therapist "should" do (just as a good actor's work is not plagued by stereotyped representations of behavior... Creative acting often shows up the absurdity of behavior based on social norms and reflexive etiquette)—it sprang afresh with each new situation and each new client. The *discipline* Fantz followed as a therapist gave her the ability to act freely and with sincerity, and yet she was utterly undogmatic; her dedication was not to a theory, but always to a situation. She used theory as a means to an end.

This creative use of theory is similar to a good actor's creative use of script. The beloved American acting teacher Sanford Meisner used to advise actors to use the words of the script as a way of expressing the flow of their own actual, underlying emotions—the flow of their actual lives while on stage. It didn't matter if the feelings didn't seem to fit the words; as long as the actor had prepared and the emotion was honest, it would infuse the playwright's text with life. In a similar way, the value of theory for a good therapist is much like the value of a script for a good actor: it's understood inside and out, but always takes a back seat to the immediate demand and inescapable reality of the actual situation. Theory directs us as to where and how to look, and in doing so provides a framework within which the unfolding experience can be understood and assimilated into an ongoing narrative for both parties. Instead of *giving* meaning, theory *points* to meaning; it is not an end in itself. Similarly, a script allows the ebb and flow of actual emotions between actual actors to become meaningful—but it isn't to be mistaken for the meaning itself. Putting theory before reality is like putting the cart before the horse. An actor's interest (and Fantz's) is always focused on the immediate, continuously unfolding engagement with the player opposite her, not on the remembered lines which she's supposed to say. She trusts that if she puts her attention where it belongs, the rest will fall into place of its own.

This faith—and the struggle which faith always entails—is what makes an actor's life on stage compelling. We've all seen players who seem to be reciting their lines by rote, without regard for the living reality of the actors around them—without regard for the context out of which their words must spring if they're to have meaning. Similarly, we've all found ourselves at times sitting with our clients and "relying too much" on theory: sounding as though we're reciting "lines" we've learned, with little regard for the uniqueness of this particular client in this particular moment. The skillful actor (like the skillful therapist) has learned how to *not stop living when she works*. The process of being in an embodied story with an other is what allows her to become *more* alive. She is interested and interesting, excited and exciting. Following Meisner's advice, she uses the words of her script (the perspectives of her theory) as supports with which to make a meaningful narrative of the unfolding experience between herself and her companion. The beginning and the end—in both theatre and psychotherapy—is the story. It tells us as we tell it, and the telling is its own reward.

Arthur Roberts
Boston, Massachusetts
Spring, 1998

PART I: ESSAYS

1
METAPHOR AND FANTASY

The concept of awareness is a basic one in the study and application of Gestalt therapy, and over the years we at the Gestalt Institute of Cleveland have evolved many different approaches to the teaching of it. We have worked with "figure-ground," with the process of widening and narrowing of focus, with differentiation and integration, and above all with the direction of attention. All of these and many others are modes that have proved very useful in the heightening of awareness.

I believe it important to stress that as we move into the realm of metaphor and fantasy we come in touch with an entirely different type of awareness, with a novel approach to authenticity. In effect we dispense in part with the cognitive function and focus instead on the intuitive part of the self.

Let me recapitulate. Awareness may be directed outward toward the external world or inward toward the self. When directed outward there are essentially two places that it may go—toward persons in the environment or objects in that same environment. When directed inward the possibilities both in direction and function are considerably broadened. It may be focused affectively on emotions or sensations or cognitively/intuitively on thoughts, memories, wishes, fantasies and metaphor.

Using the last of these as a point of departure, it's extremely exciting to me to realize that language, particularly metaphor, is not simply a means of communication but rather an "organ of perception," (Jaynes, 1976, p.51)—a way, in other words, of perceiving the world. I remember with both fondness and astonishment a ride into the country in early spring. The countryside was burgeoning, and my companion and I were surrounded on all sides by lush bushes of yellow, sunlit blooms. My friend suddenly stopped the car and pointing to the yellow dazzlement asked, "What is the name for those?" "Forsythia," I replied simply. "Oh," said he, "Forsythia! Now I can think of it."

In this particular example, yellowness, lushness, luminosity, all the qualities that forsythia encompasses, were not in themselves adequate to allow for discrimination; a name was necessary to tie them together to form a unique "gestalt" which in the future could convey a memory of yellowness, lushness, luminosity. But a label is not a metaphor. It is a means of connoting a meaning that is already specific, derived over time. Metaphor on the other hand is a special way of bestowing meaning on something novel that at one particular moment is as yet strange, unnamed, unrealized and tantalizing. Labels allow us to "think" about something we already know; metaphors permit us to "experience" something formerly unknown in the light of our previous history. In a word—to make contact.

Julian Jaynes in *The Origin of Consciousness in the Breakdown of the Bicameral Mind* points out that many parts of the human body have been used as metaphors. For example, if one thinks of a "head," one may use it in a way to signify the very top of something as in the head of an army, the head of a table, the head of a bed or the head of a household. One's visage provides a cogent way of looking at or speaking picturesquely of things such as the face of a clock, of a cliff, of a card, of a crystal. Eyes too are often used to characterize objects in a way which gives or endows them with additional meaning, e.g. the eye of a needle, the eye of a storm, the eye of a flower. The same kind of effect can be produced by utilizing "teeth." We speak of the teeth of a comb, the teeth of an argument, the teeth of a gale—all of these implying bite and power without the necessity for amplification.

The skin too is an important metaphor. How often have you heard people say, "Stay in touch" with individuals who are "thick skinned," or "thin-skinned," or "touchy?" How often have you, yourself, said "Handle him carefully lest you 'rub' him the wrong way?" We speak of "feeling" for another person; we speak of "touching" experience. All of these expressions derive from our own sense of touch and that of those who have gone before us to the first syllable of recorded time.

In very early times language and its referents climbed up from the concrete to the abstract on the steps of metaphor. Our commonly used verb form "to be" derives from the Sanskrit word "asmi" which signifies "to breathe." Interestingly, eons ago there was no word for "existence." One breathed or one grew or one essentially *was not*. Every conscious thought can be traced, if we try diligently enough, through metaphor, back to concrete actions in a concrete world (Jaynes, 1976). For example, "my runaway thoughts" is an expression which emanates from the explicit action, "to run." To be very specific, understanding a thing, any thing—any person—is to arrive at a metaphor for that thing or person by substituting something more familiar. The feeling of familiarity is the feeling of understanding.

I'm reminded of my nephew gingerly holding his sister's new-born son for the first time—clearly uncomfortable, unable to relax. And as the little one squirmed about and screwed up his face, my nephew said, "Oh, what a little monkey you are!" and suddenly smiled and was at ease. Out of strangeness—familiarity.

It was not the naming that was crucial here but the qualities that the name evoked—those qualities of playfulness, wrinkledness, slipperiness, smallness—that brought to the unknown a kind of recognition, without which there could have been no acceptance, no immediate joy.

When we consider metaphor and fantasy, it is crucial to be aware that we possess a complete apperceptive mass from which these metaphors, these fantasies originate. I am reminded of Rilke's notion of living fully before sitting down to write. Our apperceptive mass is what we refer to in Gestalt terms as "background," our assimilated experience out of which new and surprising "figures" may continually emerge. It is composed of all that we have read in our lifetimes. It can range from history to myths. When I think of history, I thing of the Fall of Troy (the beautiful Helen, the enamored Paris and, of course, the unforgettable Trojan Horse), I think of Ghengis Khan and the Asiatic hoards over-running Europe, of the Spanish Inquisition and the Spanish Conquest, of the discovery of America and its settlement, of the French Revolution replete with Marie Antoinette's, "Let them eat cake!" and the guillotine, of the first and second world wars and the fall of the atom bomb on Hiroshima.

When I reflect on some of the literature I have enjoyed I recollect *Crime and Punishment, The Brothers Kharomazov, The Scarlet Letter, Moby Dick, Wuthering Heights,* and more lately the spy novels of John Le Carre. These oeuvres color the way I think, the way I see, just as what you may have enjoyed colors your perspective.

If I turn to fairy tales I become very conscious of how often they involve Jungian archetypes—the wicked step mother or witch, the innocent child, the ideal hero, the polarities of good and evil.

And myths—the stories of a hero or heroine beset by temptation, tests of the self, universal struggle. Jason and the Golden Fleece immediately leap to mind. How unforgettable are the fire-breathing bulls, the sowing of the dragon's teeth which immediately sprouted from an armed guard, and the aid received from the sorceress, Medea. How memorable the *Iliad,* the Homeric counterpart to the Fall of Troy. Interestingly, Jaynes cited the *Iliad* as an example of great writing which existed before the development of the conscious mind. Nowhere in the poem (in the original Greek) do its characters think, ponder, decide: rather Odysseus, Agamemnon and Achilleus respond *in action* to the "voices of the Gods."

Our apperceptive mass may also include the music we've heard. This music may range from the great classics of Bach,

Beethoven, and Brahms, through folk songs, blues and jazz, to
modern rock and such cult creations as the Rocky Horror Picture
Show which my daughter, Lori, saw 26 times, memorizing in the
process every one of the songs, replete with the accent and style of
the varied singers. One of my former group members had the
uncanny ability to hum or sing out in the middle of a session some
show tune or symphonic theme which metaphorically represented
precisely where another member was emotionally or otherwise. It
cut through a lot of crap.

Our metaphors may emerge from the art we have
perceived, from the softness of line and color of a Renoir, from
the angularity and strangeness of color of a Picasso, the depth and
richness of color of a Rembrandt—who has ever seen the Man in
the Golden Helmet and could not make it a part of himself?—the
freshness of color and piquancy of shape of a Miro. The list is
endless.

They may also derive from the architecture we have
viewed, from the clean strong lines of modern buildings, the
gingerbread forms of the Victorian era, from the Acropolis to a
Howard Johnson Motel. They may derive from all things seen in
nature: a turbulent stream, a corkscrew willow, the magnificence
of the Grand Canyon or the breathtaking sight of a deer, ears up,
poised for flight.

In short, our apperceptive mass includes all of those
"figures" I've mentioned above, plus all those you may name—
and in addition the experiences in our lives of birth, death, pain,
joy, power and loss. Out of these do metaphors grow. In essence
they emanate from the depths of our learning and the richness or
paucity of our culture.

In addition, the use of metaphor is a process of translation
from the lengthy and ordinary to the cogent and pithy. Not only is
it a short-cut to communication but it is a representation of
awareness in image form. Metaphor, to look at it in a slightly
different but related way, has its roots in Freud's idea of primary
process. To review, the "primary process" was, or is, if you will,

37

the way in which infants tried to discharge tension by forming images of the object that would remove their tension. For example, a hungry infant might "image" or conjure up a picture of food or of the mother's breast which might be a fount of milk. (I am not referring here to "primary process" as Perls *et al* uses it when they speak of health as primary process in contact, but rather as Perls himself might have used it when he was more immediately influenced by psychoanalysis.) This "image" of the infant is not, as I think of it, pure fantasy as it might be in the adult, but more precisely an actual "experiencing" which, unfortunately for the infant, does *not* lead to satisfaction.

Since the primary process alone cannot actually reduce tension (one cannot eat a mental image), the secondary process begins to develop, and the ego—the second system of the personality—begins to form. It is essential in development, certainly. But unfortunately we as a species get so carried away by the secondary process that we lose touch with our images; we get lost in the world of words, of ever rational thought. Perhaps it is time to return—at least for moments—to the primary process, to the time before labeling began, to allow our images to give us direction.

We meet someone whose long blond hair evokes images of Rapunzel, the princess in the tower, the need to rescue. These images which contain qualities that make for metaphor may afford an opening to feelings about the person in the here and now. It becomes possible to move with these feelings guided by our metaphor.

In somewhat the same way we can move with our fantasies; we can urge our clients into directed awareness, directed fantasy (a way to catch awareness at unawares). There are many ways in which to do this, but I will mention two of the most simple, and perhaps most familiar. The first one is to suggest to a client or a group, "Go into a cave and tell me what you find there." In actuality this statement is preceded by some minimally mesmerizing sentences such as, "You are walking along a twisting wooded path with the sun shining slant-wise through the gold leaves of the aspens. A slight breeze is blowing so that the fragile leaves shiver making a silvery, whispering sound. The wild flowers along the way brighten the pathway with flashes of iridescent, luminous color. Suddenly you come to a clearing and see looming before you the dark entrance to a cave. Go into that cave, and tell me what you see."

When this directed fantasy trip is attempted in a group—training or therapeutic—many of the students come up with spontaneous and variegated responses. I've encountered gold filled streams, cold pools of dark water, mud, wolves, bears, bats, Formica speckled rock and occasionally, nothing. If I know my group, it's intriguing to discover how often the fantasies which individuals dream up are apt metaphors for parts of themselves.

Similarly, when I work with individuals, the directed fantasy can be amazingly effective in furthering the therapeutic process. I vividly recall engaging with an extremely attractive woman, always nice to a fault but with a facade that was utterly impenetrable. Upon being asked to go into the ubiquitous cave, she approached it in fantasy, and then drew back in alarm, saying she couldn't possible enter it, that it frightened her. After dealing partially with her fear, I asked her to describe the cave to me. She did so with some reluctance. It was seen by her as a dark, towering side of a mountain, smooth surfaced like granite and quite impenetrable. I asked her whether it had any opening, since caves usually do, and she replied that it did but the opening was blocked by a huge boulder which she could not budge. Asked to see if she could find some sort of tool to help her get some leverage, she finally discovered an iron crowbar with which she began to pry aside the boulder—about one inch. At which point she looked at me and said, "I am like that cave; I've made myself smooth and unapproachable—even to myself. Not only do I not want others to have access to me, but I'm afraid to look inside myself." So for the moment we stopped. I respected her reluctance; but in further sessions we did enter her cave to discover much of richness there.

The second directed fantasy we frequently use is the one in which we ask a client or a group "to dig a hole and bring out and describe what is buried there." The preamble to this can be very similar to the one which precedes the request to go into a cave. By the same token, the responses to the suggestion—both from the group or the individual client—vary in much the same way as did those to the first experiment. Even the resistances bear a certain similitude. What might you find if you dug a hole? How might you resist digging it?

Once again I am reminded of an individual client of mine who would sit with me week after week on my same gold love seat and parsimoniously proffer pieces of her existence, rarely without extreme investment of energy from me. Needless to say, though I was quite interested in who and what she was, I was also exceedingly frustrated. It's significant to the playing out of her fantasy that in appearance she was very handsome and tall, with straight red hair pulled tightly back, richly though very simply dressed, and in manner, taciturn, stern, almost hard.

When I asked her to dig a hole, she looked at me as if I might have one in my head, eventually started, with huge reluctance, to wander through the rocky field I'd invented for her, and stopped almost immediately because she had nothing with which to dig. With some additional coaxing she at last found a sturdy stick with which she could begin to scratch the surface of the ground. Actually she dug and dug, stopping intermittently to pronounce the experience silly and to complain that it was useless since she would *never* find anything. I urged her on. Suddenly an expression of utter surprise appeared on her face, and she sat bolt upright in her seat. I asked what had happened, and she replied, "But I have something!" I asked her to bring it up and show it to me, and with much reticence she leaned towards me as if to hand me a rather heavy object. I did not take it but suggested instead that she look at it herself and tell me about it. It turned out to be a book, very dusty, covered with dirt having been buried so long a time. But when she brushed the dirt away, she said, "Oh—it's so lovely; it's covered with the softest of blue leather, the pages are edged with gilt as though they must have much of importance written on them, and the huge volume is bound with golden clasps as if there's much of richness inside." As of course there was. She had made her own metaphor.

I could give you many more examples, even delve into the realm of the undirected fantasy, but I'd like to close simply with a quote from Highet.

> We are all cave-men. The cave we inhabit is our own mind, and consciousness is like a tiny torch, flickering and flaring, which can at best show us only a few outlines of the cave-wall that stands nearest, or reflect a dangerous underground river flowing noiselessly at our feet, so that we start back in horror before we are engulfed; as we explore, we come often on shapes of beauty, glittering stalagtites, jewel encrusted pillars, delicate and trusting animals... (Highet, 1954, p.36)

And so we do, if we allow ourselves our fantasies, our metaphors, our dreams.

41

2

THE GESTALT APPROACH TO DREAMS

The Gestalt theory of dreams derives organically from the body of Gestalt principles and methodology and is perhaps most representative of the differences which exist between the existential modes of therapy and the more traditional procedures. Two concepts which are central to the understanding of Gestalt formulations are the idea of need fulfillment as a process of progressive formation and destruction of gestalten and that of differentiation and integration as exemplified by the work with polarities.

The notion of need fulfillment is a familiar one, encountered in many theories of psychology ranging from Freud to Rogers to Maslow, and differing chiefly in the importance granted to the specified needs. Perls' view of the patterning of needs was one of constant flux or movement; he did not see any one or two needs as preeminent, nor did he view them as necessarily hierarchical. Rather, he regarded them as a function of shifts in a figure-ground relationship. As one need becomes figural, perceived, paid attention to, expressed and satisfied, it promptly becomes destroyed or destructured, that is, returned to the ground from which it came, and another need is then able to emerge, become figural and organize the individual's perceptual field into a new and energizing form. In the integrated individual this process from formation to destruction of gestalten proceeds smoothly with little or no interruption. New figures are always

43

being formed. When the needs which regulate their formation are satisfied, they are destructured and new ones arise. It is only when the needs are blocked, repressed or not recognized that they cannot be discharged and so remain—not quite figure, not quite ground—to muddy the individual's perceptual field and prevent the emergence of a new need which might organize the field in a cogent and coherent manner. It is the task of Gestalt therapy to make these blocked, repressed, unrecognized needs more flowing, conscious, reowned.

One of the chief modes of actuating this phenomenon is through the concept of polarities. Polar traits—or, more simply, opposing traits—in the individual may be viewed as dualities which fight and paralyze one another. But it is more viable to regard them as a starting pint for the potential integration of the total personality. Perls' paramount philosophy—indeed, that of Gestalt therapy—is one of differentiation and integration. Analysis as a modus operandi for the growth and development of latent power remains inadequate since it reduces all behavior to its smallest denominator and neglects the synthesis that would result in a more meaningful whole. The woman who has been in analysis for ten years only to discover after laborious and minute introspection that her problems in social intercourse stem from her early absorption in masturbation has no tools with which to improve her social intercourse. On the other hand, the attempt to integrate polar traits by first separating them out, recognizing them as one's own in spite of their often paradoxical appearance an assimilating them in some compromise form, or as parts of the self that are appropriate to different life situations rather than as stereotyped or stimulus-response kinds of reactions, allows one to evolve a more comprehensive whole as well as a more suitable behavioral patterning. Instead of the individual refusing to confront particular needs because they are ostensibly contradictory to other needs which feel more ego-syntonic, he is able to allow room in his ever-expanding system of self for myriads of needs which, if expressed, can elicit from his environment sufficient nourishment to allow for increasing development.

Bearing in mind, then, the concept of the need fulfillment pattern of the individual as a process of Gestalt formation and destruction and the concept of polarities as a process of differentiation and integration, we find ourselves possessed of a conceptual framework for the theory of dreams.

Unlike the Freudians, who regard dream work as an attempt to disguise the workings of the psyche and who consequently cut up the dreams into their component parts, which are then assigned a symbolic meaning, the same meaning for every individual—unlike the Freudians, who then resort to association and interpretation as a means of understanding the dream, the Gestalt therapist views the dream as an existential message from the dreamer, a means of creative expression, much as a painting, a poem or a choreographic fantasy is a creative expression, which allows the dreamer to come into touch with the very personal, idiosyncratic parts of his being.

It is important to remember that Gestalt therapy, and dream work as a part of that therapy, is an existential and phenomenological approach to the study of human behavior. It is inextricably anchored in the here and now; the only reality occurs where I am in this moment of time, and in this here and this now I am the ongoing process—never static, always becoming. And in this process, I move from the awareness to the satisfaction to the destruction of my constantly forming needs. Only when this flow is interrupted do I become static, confused, steeped in pathology. This "stuckness," this pathology, is clearly manifested in dreams as a part of the total existence of the dreamer.

A very important function of the existential message of the dream is to present to the dreamer the "holes" in his personality. These present themselves in the dream as voids, or empty spaces. They present themselves as avoidances or as objects or persons with whom it is impossible or fear-provoking to identify. In other words, the dream work calls attention to those

45

needs in the individual which have not been met because they have not been recognized. So the need fulfillment pattern is interrupted, and as a consequence we have recurrent dreams, often nightmarish in quality, which will continue to clutter up the dreamer's sleeping field until they are confronted.

Perls maintains that *everything* is in a dream—the existential difficulty, the missing and therefore limiting part of the personality, as well as the fully integrated and identified part of the self. The dream can be seen as a central attack directly into the midst of one's nonexistence. And as such it is a marvelous tool, a catalyst for becoming.

Now, the mechanism most central to the Gestalt theory of dreams is that of projection. And like the various other resistances to contact, it may be viewed in its pathological sense and in its creative functioning. Pathologically, projection is seen as an impulse which by rights belongs to one's own organism or behavioral system but is disowned and put out into the environment, where it is then experienced as directed against the self by some person or object—usually forcefully. Creatively, projection serves as basis for empathy inasmuch as we can identify in others only those qualities or emotions we have experienced ourselves. At its most inventive, projection is the source of all artistry—music, drama, painting, dance.

Another way of looking at this dichotomy, this division into pathological and creative projection, is to consider the projections as part projections as opposed to whole projections. The part projections, incomplete and fragmentary, are pathological. They stem from introjects which have not been thoroughly digested nor spit up, but rather remain as painful lumps in the psyche until they are projected out into the world. Let us take the example of the youngster who has introjected the judgmentalism of his stern but loving father. He is not comfortable with this judgmentalism, and, disliking it in his father, he will not accept it in himself. But the impulse toward judging is there, and so he attributes it to others in his world whom he then resents. The important thing to remember is that it is the judgmentalism, the undigested introject, which is projected, rather than the *totality* of the stern but *loving* father. If on the other hand, the youngster grown to manhood can accept and understand in his father and in himself the sternness, the judgmentalism and the loving nature that comprise, along with many other qualities, the substance of their respective characters, he conceivably could create a novel which might utilize all the knowledge of fathers and sons garnered from intimate experience. This is the total projection, which fosters artistic endeavor, which allows for the total identification of the self with the other. Total projection is of necessity aware projection, projection that is deliberate and focused rather than capricious and sporadic—in a word, the very opposite of pathological.

In Gestalt therapy we view dreams as projections—not only pathological ones in which the impulse is disowned and consequently projected onto the environment from which it in turn plagues the self, but aware, creative projections which pit the individual's recognized and identified facets against his repudiated ones in a confrontation which can lead to discovery and knowledge. The sleeping state of the dreamer is regarded as an immense and unending projection screen on which projections flicker and pass. In time the totality of one's existence is formulated there. The more fragmented the individual, the more nightmarish the dreams—the more filled with holes, with avoidances, with sterility. The more well-integrated the individual, the fewer the holes—the clearer the identification, the more generative the process.

If we accept the premise that the dream incorporates both the accepted and rejected parts of the self, it then becomes an instrument for exploring and consolidating those parts of our personality that as yet remain unrealized. As long as we are able to remember our dreams, they are still alive for us and pregnant with unfinished situations—situations which remain unassimilable. Of course, the more unassimilable the situations,

47

the less likely we are to remember the dream and the more apt we are to be phobic. Those people who refuse to remember their dreams are, in essence, refusing to face their existence.

When Perls first began his work with dreams, he was content to have the dreamer speak of himself as each of the myriad parts of the dream. For example, if I dreamed of a red and orange afghan made of expensive wool, I might describe myself as soft, sumptuous and colorful, both a comfort to the touch and a delight to the eye. If, on the other hand, I dreamed of a black granite-topped table, I could describe myself as dark and cold, indestructible and perhaps useful for holding things.

As he delved deeper and deeper into the substance of dreams and their efficacy in effecting change and growth in the personality, Perls came to believe that it was essential for the dreamer not only to delineate himself verbally as the parts of the dream but to play out all the parts *actively*. Only through the playing out of the parts could any real identification take place. And it is this very identification that is a counteraction to the alienation that had been in existence. "That's not me, that's something else, something strange, something not belonging to me."

Central to Perls' trend toward a more active approach to the dream was the notion held by Hefferline and Goodman, as well as himself, that in this age of alienation the individual made *things* out of his own behavior, his own processes. Rather than functioning creatively, "creativity" becomes a dream to talk about; instead of vitally moving from experience to experience, "vitality" becomes a *cause célèbre*. As a consequence of never experiencing himself in action, man divests himself of the responsibility for those very actions. Even his language becomes impersonal and empty of ownership. "It's sad that he had to die" replaces "I am sad, and I am lonely." "There's a tightness in my stomach" substitutes for "I'm holding myself tight and giving myself a pain in my gut!"

By getting the dreamer to identify *actively* with each part of his dream, by inducing him to project himself *totally* into his alienated facets so that he in verity becomes that thing, that afghan, that granite tabletop, the dreamer is forced ultimately to reown, reintergrate and finally take responsibility for the sum of his existence. If I in turn were to become my afghan in action, I might drape myself over the legs or shoulders of someone in a group or the someone to whom I am telling my dream. In so doing I might come in contact not only with my own warmth but with the warmth—or coldness—of the person I touched. I might experience myself as instrumental in changing the physical or emotional temperature of someone else in the world. I might experience my power. If, on the other hand, I become my black, granite-topped table, I might actively stiffen up and discover how rigidly I force myself to hold back if I wish to keep myself dark and cold and unresponsive. I might discover the amount of energy I force myself to expend in the maintenance of a hard surface rather than an open vulnerability. I might be better able to assess the cost to myself of an unthinking way of being.

In this way the dreamer can experience his own reality much as Van Den Berg came to appreciate the reality of his patients through their view of their own worlds—through the phenomenological here and now. If one of his patients describes the people in the street as "hostile, meaningless puppets," who are separated from him by huge distances even though they brush against him in passing, Van Den Berg recognized that this distance is the only way in which the patient experiences the presence of other people. He projects his own need for distance, his own hostility into the world around him. So, too, do I project my own warmth, softness, coldness, darkness into my dreams.

On the face of it, this process—the process of identifying with and reclaiming our own holes, our own rejected parts— seems simple enough. The paramount goal of the individual—at least in the eyes of Perls, Maslow, Rogers, May and certainly Goldstein, who believe it's the only motive that the organism

49

possesses—is that of self-actualization. "Any need is a deficit state which motivates the person to replenish the deficit. It is like a hole that demands to be filled in. This replenishment or fulfillment of a need is what is meant by self-actualization." Unfortunately, the process of self-actualization, of becoming what we have the potential to become, is fraught with difficulty only partly of our own making. The individual happily and unhappily does not live in a vacuum. He lives instead in the teeming vortex of what we term "society." And it is when our own individual needs for becoming come into conflict with society's need for conformity and the status quo that we find ourselves at an impasse.

One way of viewing this impasse is to regard it as a pause in the maturation process. As we become more mature, more adult, we move from environmental supports to self-supports, or from obsolete self-supports to those that are more authentic or current. However, when environmental supports cease to exist, and self-supports, not fully developed, are insufficient to sustain the necessary activity of being in the world, we stumble, we panic, we freeze. We discover that our introjections, those pieces of our early environment that we've swallowed whole without assimilating, are forcing us into repetitive and stereotyped modes of behaving; our repressions, which in Gestalt theory are viewed as comprised of muscular phenomena or motor processes, are forcing us into muscular contractions which prevent flowing movement and at their worst cause us to develop body symptoms and joint involvements. In other words, those resistances to contact which we have afforded ourselves in order to cope with the anxiety that is evoked by refusing to move from excitement to action are proving to be ineffective, difficult and painful to maintain.

These pauses in the maturation process can be easily identified in dreams. One can see, for example, that part of the dream that is representative of the drive toward self-actualization. It could be something as obvious as running freely and easily in a sun-warmed meadow. One can see that part of the dream that depicts society's dictum to conform—something as simple as dreaming of oneself as part of a regiment clothed in uniforms that are absolutely identical.

Our introjections can be recognized through the identification of a mother figure or a father figure in a dream, by a policeman, by a judge. Our repressions can be perceived by difficulties in identification with persons who possess traits which we regard antipathetically—persons who are miserly, avaricious, hostile, self-pitying. The refusal to acknowledge these traits can do nothing to dissolve them. Only by reclaiming them, exaggerating them, becoming them in action can we assimilate them and so utilize them appropriately. After all, each of us can conceive of times when it might be advantageous and possibly powerful to be miserly, avaricious, hostile or self-pitying.

I would like to emphasize again that in our dream work it is not enough to recognize the parts of the dream or even to claim as one's own the characteristics which these fragments represent. It is vital to actually become in *action* one's myriad facets. It is imperative to *move* as does one's dream image, to use one's voice to sound one's moods, to sound whispery and seductive as the houri, to shout loudly and bombastically as the demagogue, to let one's voice break as the small child who has been punished or rejected. Only thus can one get in touch with the stark reality of those parts of the self.

Not only is it important to act out these manifestations of the self, it is revealing and exciting to develop scripts and to set the stage for a confrontation between two parts of the self that incorporate polar traits. The moment one parcels out opposing characteristics, and develops a dialogue between them—the moment these dissimilar and often disowned facets meet, not only do they become vivid and compelling, but an ascendancy of one part over another becomes whining and self-deprecatory. One can capture the flavor of strength in the self that resists the autocratic manipulation and help kindle it into an effective, potent force in the dreamer's life field. By calling attention to the phenomenon of the immediate happening, the therapist can aid the dreamer in discovering how he uses his various parameters, in discovering what needs to be further developed or enriched, what needs to be argued with or cajoled into moving over temporarily, what needs to be recognized as obsolete, nonprofitable and interfering with one's maximum function.

If one continues to fight those parts of the self which one disparages, if one refuses to take responsibility for them and does not allow them to be incorporated, assimilated into the self, these parts will continue to exist—but chaotically and not subject to our rational control. They will appear when least useful and most inappropriate rather than as a part of a unified, acknowledged self that functions smoothly and appropriately and in a vital and exciting fashion.

In his later years, Perls used the working of dreams almost exclusively as his therapeutic approach, relying on the experience achieved by the dreamer in acting out the multiple dream fragments as revelatory and growth-producing. Most of the Gestalt therapists with whose work I am familiar count on dream work as an important part of their armamentorium, but none of them use it exclusively. I, myself, move in cycles, sometimes devoting numerous therapy sessions to the exploration of dreams, sometimes never engaging a client in them at all. My reasons vary. With certain individuals there may be so much happening in the here and now that I am presented with a plethora of richness and feel no need to go on additional fishing expeditions. With others, though I would welcome the richness that accompanies the dream work, I find them extremely resistant to working a dream if they have one: "It's too silly; I'll feel like an idiot; it's childish!" Or, "I never dream, and if I do, I never remember them."

When a client is resistant to dreaming but still presents viable areas from his life space to pursue in therapy, I may never insist that she remember her dreams. This stems from some laziness on my part inasmuch as coaxing a non-cooperative dreamer to first dream and then explore her dreams is really quite difficult work. However, if a client has reached a point in therapy where she is by no means at the point of termination but is stuck in a morass of non-communication both with herself and with me, then I insist that she dream. I insist that she dream since everyone dreams, that she remember her dreams since one may do this merely by *not* moving one's head from the pillow, that she write down her dreams since anyone can put out a pad and a pencil before sleeping, and that she bring the dreams in with her to her next therapy session. She will.

It is not necessary that the dream be a complete three-act production. As a matter of fact, the longer the dream, the more difficult it is to engage it thoroughly since the therapy hour is limited. A very short dream, or even a dream fragment, can be most effective as a pathway to the hidden or disowned self. The important thing is to avoid getting sucked into the client's deprecating statements that the dream is too short or too undefined to be of value.

Very early in therapy with a twenty-six-year-old, shy, diffident, nonverbal man who, not unnaturally, had trouble communicating and often spoke in huge generalizations, he had his first dream. Say, rather, a dream fragment. He reported waking up early one morning tearing at his arms—he had a skin allergy which troubled him intermittently—with the word "around" in his head left over from a dream. I asked him to try to think of himself in some way as "a round," two words. He finally thought of himself as a circle, more particularly as being inside a circle and trying to scratch his way out. He then thought of himself as in a spotlight, a *round* spotlight. I asked him how he thought of this, and he replied, "When my skin's pretty bad, I think I look damn lousy. I give myself nicknames like 'Itchy, Goomey, Scratch.' And I remember how a kid in the lunchroom when I was a child got sick when he watched me scratch. It didn't make me feel so good. I'm uncomfortable shopping by myself, having to face somebody. I break out in a cold sweat from simple embarrassment." Now, this was the first time he had ever referred to his skin in therapy and the first time he had acknowledged the embarrassment that was manifest during interviews with me. He would squirm in his chair, rarely look at me and smile inappropriately down at his hands, which were red and raw. After he had shared his dream fragment with me, he was occasionally able to look at me. In effect, he had given me entree into his *circle,* from which most of the world was excluded.

I could, of course, have had the young man be his circle; I could have had him position himself as one with his hands around his feet and his head down and turned away from the world, and so have him experience his closed-offness, his inability to see anything outside of himself. I could have had him exaggerate that turning away and experience the tightness of it and the energy needed to maintain that position. But it was early in the therapeutic process, and his way of getting in touch with himself, his world and me was more than adequate for where we were in that moment of time—and not so threatening. It is important to gauge an individual's readiness for experimentation and to move him toward the cutting edge of growth without causing him to take on risks for which he has as yet no supports.

Given, then, that I have as a client someone who generously or reluctantly presents me with his dream productions, how do we proceed clinically from manifest dream content to self-disclosure?

I ask him to start very simply by relating to me his dream in the first person and in the present tense, as if it were happening here and now for the very first time. By doing this, he virtually gets into the mood of the dream and finds it difficult to objectify it or to relate it as a story which does not pertain to himself. The actual telling of the dream in this fashion will often get the dreamer in touch with some important aspect of himself that eluded him while merely writing down the dream.

The next step for the dreamer is to actively become the different parts of the dream. I'm often asked, "What part do you start with?" "How do you choose among the manifold facets?" There are various ways. Sometimes I will ask a client to try to become that part of the dream which is invested with the most energy. This is a useful place because it quickly does away with whatever inertia may be present. On the other hand, it may be too emotionally laden for comfort, and a more neutral projection could be more comfortably portrayed. If the dream is not too long, I may suggest that the dreamer play out in order the varying parts of the dream. This has the advantage of including parts that the dreamer might otherwise neglect because he thought them unimportant or because he found it difficult to identify with them. It is of great moment that those parts of ourselves which we cannot or will not claim be dealt with, because they represent the holes in our personalities, our unrealized potential.

Say, for example, that a person dreams of an octopus and that he can in no way conceive of himself in that role. No problem. If he cannot see how he is like the octopus, he can express all the ways his is *unlike* the octopus. For example, "I am not dark; I am not ugly; I do not grab at things and people and squeeze the life out of them; I am not frightening; I am not rubbery." The important question to ask is, "Never?" On exploration the dreamer may realize that though his skin and hair are fair, he may be subject to dark moods which he finds necessary to hide because his mother might have told him when he was sad that he was just sleepy. He may discern that though his visage is handsome or comely, his disposition is occasionally frightful and that he shuts himself away form the world rather than share his unseemly self. He might speculate while squeezing the life out of a pillow that he does not allow himself to put his two arms around any person because if he did so he might encounter his overpowering need to hold someone close for warmth or comfort or support which for him could mean a denial of his manliness. He might recognize that he is *not* frightening because he hides his black moods and his sometimes ugly disposition through the fear of rejection and that in so doing he prevents himself from truly being known and abnegates his power. And finally he might contemplate the fact that though his body is firm and often rigid rather than rubbery, allowing it to occasionally go slack or to twist in rubbery gyrations might be exciting, graceful and vulnerable. By examining closely the things which he clearly claims as his non-self, he enables himself to identify in some new way with those disclaimed attributes, to reown them, to establish his own responsibility for them and to incorporate them into his behavior system in some productive way.

A next step in the dream work is the dialogue between different aspects of the dream. The dialogue sharply illustrates the divergence present in the personality of the dreamer, his opposing goals and motivations, his early training as contrasted with his current needs, his inability at first to pay attention to what one part of him wants.

One of my clients, who is an aspiring and very talented violinist but also a wife and mother of three children, dreamed of wandering in a city full of dark, square buildings silhouetted against a sky of intense and brilliant light. After having her experience herself as both the buildings and the light, I asked her to make up a dialogue between these two aspects of her personality. As the buildings, she sat squarely on my couch with her feet firmly planted on the floor, her hands primly folded in her lap and seriously said, "I am square and solid and deeply rooted, and I want to be allowed to remain as I am." As the light, she rose to her feet and moved gracefully around the room, replying, "I am intense and brilliant and very powerful, and I am going to illuminate you!"

> Buildings: I don't want to be illuminated; I don't want to be visible to all eyes and stared at and judged—I want to remain inconspicuous and attend to my homey things.

Light: You're blocking me! You're preventing me from shining forth in full splendor; you're cutting me off.

Buildings: But you'll expose my imperfections—I don't want you to shine on me. Go away.

Light: No, I cannot extinguish my brilliance and leave you to your lethargy! I have a need to express myself, a need to expose you, let you be seen.

Buildings: But you would expose my most intimate being, the insides of me as well as my outer shape. I would be vulnerable—open to the world.

Light: That's true, but you have much to share. You have a depth of feeling that you could communicate to others and warm their lives for a little. You are being stingy by hoarding your emotions and not conveying them in your music.

Buildings: I hear some of what you're saying, but you scare me a little. I don't know what I would lose.

Light: You might lose your rootedness, some of your concrete foundation, but you could share my freedom, my limitlessness, my intensity, my power.

Buildings: Some of what you say sounds very attractive. Maybe I could let you illuminate me a little. I

would really like to plumb my intimacy and
share it in a meaningful way.

Light: What you really should do is go to the beach
           and just lie in the sun and absorb all my
           warmth into you.

Buildings: Oh, yes!

With this exclamation, my dreamer grew rosy red almost
as if she had been sitting in the sun, and her face was lovely and
relaxed and illuminated.

Now, both of these aspects of the dreamer were not
unknown to her. She had talked about them dispassionately many
times, but the look of her as she became her light, the vibrancy in
her voice as she spoke, the freedom with which she moved
allowed her to experience this dimension of herself with an
immediacy that effectively communicated with her more stolid,
wife-mother entrenched self and loosened its position as an
obstacle toward growth.

This particular dream vividly illustrates the importance of
the setting of the dream, the place where the action begins to
emerge. Phenomenologically, my violinist sees her world as a
place of tremendous energy and light. She sees life as an
illuminated experience made up in part of shelter, in part of
sharing and exposure. It is possible to lift from the setting of any
dream one view of the dreamer's world in microcosm. Life is a
theater, life is a merry-go-round, life is a wake, a dull and dreary
void, a Christmas tree loaded with presents. And it may be any of
these things at any one point in time and all of them ultimately.
What the dream does is say, "Here's where I am now, today, this
minute. And here is the place from which I must move."

Clinically, then, the dream may be used to enable the
client to encounter both the alienated and accepted parts of the
self, to rediscover lost areas and develop neglected ones, to

redefine both one's self and one's objectives through open and impactful interchange between the fragments of the self in dialogue, and to recognize one's statement of one's own existence.

In addition, it may present a vehicle for communication with the therapist and an instrument for the elimination of paranoid projections which may abound. If the therapist is merely the recipient of the dream, it is very possible that the dreamer may experience him eventually as a voyeur and try to close him out of his world. Carl Whitaker, to counteract this, used an approach which he termed "forced fantasy." In this, he had the dreamer invent a role for the therapist in the dream. Often when a dream appears unfinished, I will ask a client to complete it in fantasy and to involve me somehow in the outcome of the dream. Needless to say, I sometimes meet up with unrecognizable views of myself. One of my clients dreamed that she was walking along a lonely stretch of beach immersed in her inward musings and conscious only of the savage pounding of the surf. She was at that time closed off in a rather sterile world unlit by human companionship which she tended to discourage by her impenetrable facade. I asked her to continue the dream with me in it as another solitary stroller and continue to move from there. She then had us approach each other in the sand and both of us pass each other by, eyes averted. I was astounded. I was tremendously fond of this particular woman and sad that she apparently was unaware of my feeling. I asked her to role-play the meeting in the sand with me. In so doing, I was able to convey the real pleasure that I experienced in meeting her in a place full of loneliness and beauty, and she was able to express to me with her tears the meaning this had for her. An impactful and exciting experience.

So far, I have discussed dream therapy in the Gestalt mode as a one-on-one experience. Potent as it is, this is not the only approach. Dream work in a group can be not only powerful for the dreamer but revelatory to the individuals in the group who play out the various roles. Joseph Zinker calls this group participation "Dreamwork as theater," and indeed it is. There are various ways of setting the stage. The dreamer may be the director and cast the parts according to his own perceptions of the people participating. He may take one of the parts for himself or merely orchestrate the others, calling for more violence, more passion, less closeness, less antagonism—stopping the play to better delineate a role as he sees it or to catch his breath as the visual and auditory happenings move him.

Another way to cast the parts is to have each member of the group—including the dreamer—choose to be a part of the dream that he feels lies closest to his own mode of being and to have the therapist direct the production in such a way as to make it most potent. Whether or not the group members pick their own roles, there is always something that may be garnered from the acting out of the dream. We are each one of us a part of the human community and as such share in the archetypes that contribute to the manifest dream. We all share in the power, the weakness, the glory and the degradation that permeates the body of a dream. Even when the elements cast are not human, even when they are in truth "elemental," we can get in touch with some of our basic ways of feeling and behaving as we act out our scripts.

In a recent workshop I did, one of the participants, a priest who was having huge conflicts about remaining in the priesthood, had a dream which shook him to his very foundations. He dreamed that he was alone in the center of a torrential storm. The rain was beating down, the lightning was flashing and the thunder rending. The wild waves beat and clamored against the shore, and the darkness cast its pall over the land.

He was ambivalent about acting out the dream in the group. One part of him was very eager to explore all the avenues of meaning, whereas another part of him was most anxious about making contact with the clearly over-powering aspects of his being. He finally decided to play himself in the dream and to parcel out the other roles among various members of the workshop. Two of the women were designated as rain, a man and a woman as lightning, two men as thunder, a man and woman as the waves, one tall, serious-minded man as the darkness, and a man and two women as the ground. I was a part of the ground as well as the director, inasmuch as the dreamer wanted to experience the full impact of the onslaught. I got the raindrops to pitter-patter at the beginning and gradually to increase in sound and fury and to hurl themselves at the dreamer in the height of the storm. The two lightnings flung themselves about in forked movements, lashing in and out of the melee, while the thunder rumbled and roared, soaring in a crescendo above the head of the crouching dreamer, who was desperately holding onto the three bodies which comprised the ground. The waves threw themselves bodily at the ground and at the dreamer attached to it, then rose and fell away, only to return in greater violence. Through the entire action the ground rested steadily and sturdily unmoving, while the darkness, coat thrown over his head as a cape, hovered closely over the dreamer, rain, lightning, thunder, waves, and ground. The sound in the room was deafening, the movement was unrestrained, and the dreamer, rocklike throughout, was never swept away.

The effect of the production on the entire company was powerful. All the moving players got in touch with their potency, their potential for violence, wildness and freedom. The man who played the darkness particularly enjoyed his ability to push down on others and to resist being pushed down in turn. And the dreamer, though he could acknowledge each of the players as a reification of his own projections, could also accept himself as able to maintain both control and solidity in the face of manifold emotions. This discovery was of profound significance to him inasmuch as it signified an ability to make rational decisions although buffeted by strong passions. A very good thing to know.

Very well, then, given that we can get a person to remember his dreams, to identify both in words and action with manifold parts of his dream, to engage in a dialogue between the

61

polarized traits of the dream and even to play out the dream as one actor in a group of peers, we discover that we have a peerless tool for the exploration of the developing self.

Dream work extends the boundary of the self, allows those shadowy parts barely perceptible or totally invisible to be experienced, tried on for size in a low-risk situation, and subsequently developed into full-blown parts of the personality. In the process the rigid structure of "character," so stultifying to full expression, is destroyed.

3
BODY LANGUAGE

I believe it was Freud who said that it was impossible to lie in psychotherapy because even though the words might be believed, the body would play one false. It is important not only for the therapist but for the patient himself to be aware of lack of congruence between the words being used, how they are used, and the bodily attitudes. I cannot tell you how many times I've listened to people telling me how important it is to them that I know all about them while at the same time they sit hunched back in their chairs with their legs tightly crossed and their hands covering their mouths or their genitals. (Notice how you are sitting at this particular moment.) I find it difficult to entirely accept their words when their bodies are very plainly telling me that they are trying to stay as closed off and protected as possible. Sooner or later I will suggest that they notice their position, their legs or their hands and that they decipher the messages that they are usually unknowingly sending out. Needless to say, the first thing that most people do is change their position—quickly. Observations are almost universally regarded as criticisms—as often they are.

Body language need not be gross in order to be understood; all sorts of important cues may be gleaned from very small muscular movements. But again the movement in itself, just as the words in themselves, cannot always be taken at face value. Muscles, as we know, are repressors as well as expressers, and the smile which appears at first glance to be projecting humor or even happiness may easily be a mask for despair or a desperate attempt to hold the face together. If you are really observant—aware, if

63

you will—you will come quickly to sense that which is incongruent and in need of further exploration.

It might be of value at this point to reexamine what Wilhelm Reich described as the segments of the body armor. Interestingly, he pointed out that these segments did not coincide with nerve paths or blood vessels as might have been expected but coincided instead with emotionally significant regions of the body. These regions are seven in number and consist of the ocular, the oral, the neck, the chest, the diaphragmatic, the abdomen, and the pelvic segments.

When Reich speaks of armor, he is speaking more concretely of immobilization. In the ocular armor he alludes to the contraction and immobilization of most muscles of the eyeballs, the lids, the forehead and the tear glands. This is expressed in the empty expression of the eyes or protruding eyeballs, a waxlike expression on both sides of the nose so that the eyes look out from a rigid mask. Even the forehead may be without expression as if "flattened out". People with this particular immobilization sometimes have been unable to cry for many years. There are those who are aware of this and who find it a painful deprivation.

A young man whom I had seen only three times in therapy had referred many times to his anger, even his rage, toward his parents who had coldly rejected him. But his expression could hardly have been called enraged; his forehead was smooth, his eyes half closed and his mouth slightly smiling. My assumption was that behind the rage, which he could admit to but not express, lurked tremendous grief or hurt. I got him to try opening his eyes wide, to wrinkle his forehead and raise his eyebrows and to attempt to get with the feeling accompanying these movements. He almost immediately felt sadness, of which he had not been aware, and experienced a lump in his throat. I asked him to tell his mother (who he imagined in the chair facing him) of his sadness and how she made him sad. He did this and suddenly found tears running down his face. He was astounded and said that he had not cried in years and that it was so good, so good! He said I couldn't know how good it felt, how freeing. And he was right, because I'd never deprived myself of this particular ability.

I want to stress again how these deprivations, unaware or not, are our own doing. If we can become aware of *how we maintain* them, not *why we started* them—which often can result only in blaming the other and excusing the self—we can choose to continue them or to employ another mode of behavior.

I remember a woman that I had in a group at one time who perpetually held her eyes open wide so that they almost protruded from her head. Her expression was one of artless wonder and naiveté. What no one could figure out was the anger which she constantly evoked in the other members of the group. Almost by chance one evening another woman in the group asked her to half close her eyes. He transformation was wild. She suddenly looked angry and hard, and the words which she had disguised (though not entirely) with her little girl look suddenly became congruent with her new expression. She had been hiding her own anger for years because she was afraid of eliciting it in others—only to find the anger there for her without apparent cause. When she got into touch with her own reality, the outer reality changed. Her openly expressed anger evoked admiration though not immediate unqualified liking.

Sometimes, as in the above example, the ocular armor may be broken through by a means as simple as the lowering of the lids. Other suggestions which Reich offers are having the person open his eyes wide, as if in fright. He claims that with this gesture, "forehead and eyelids are mobilized and express emotions" (Reich, 1949, p.371). Often this includes the upper segments of the cheeks, especially if the patient grimaces and produces a grin which appears spiteful.

The second armor segment, the oral, is composed of the muscles of the chin, throat, and mouth. Emotions such as crying and expressions of angry biting, or grimacing, yelling or sucking are difficult if not impossible while the oral armor is functional. Often the expression accompanying this particular immobilization might be visible—and attended to. Again, there are ways in which the patient can be brought into contact with his armor. Any exaggerated movement of mouth or jaw, any chewing or biting motions, any grimaces—which, incidentally, will almost invariably cause your patient to feel silly and so balky—will begin to dissolve the oral armor.

There is a fascinating experiment I've used in several drama workshops which approximates the undoing of the facial armor without actually dissolving it in reality. The participants are asked to don semi-transparent masks, animal or human, through which their own faces may be partially seen. They are then told to examine themselves in a mirror provided for this purpose and to act out the character which they feel themselves to be. Some of the transformations are amazing. I particularly recall a very cool pretty girl who had behaved with tremendous reserve throughout the workshop. She selected a battered, bleeding mask with a bandage 'round the head and transformed herself into a stumbling, lewd, loose prostitute. She reported afterward that she could have never approximated the role with her own face set in its own patterns. I sincerely believed her.

I also remember a man who in two workshops (each a year apart) selected the same mask, feeling that it was the one least like himself. The mask presented a forced, stiffly amiable grin to the world, and the astounding part of the whole thing was that it fit his own smile like a glove. It was hard to tell the difference between the man in the mask and the man without the mask. He had absolutely *no* idea what he looked like. I subsequently took him on in therapy to get rid of the mask. The hidden rage was fantastic.

Very well, say we've succeeded in mobilizing the musculature in the ocular and oral segment so that the person becomes aware of his urge to cry or to shout. If the rest of his body is mobile we have no problem, but if the neck segment, for example, is still armored we're in trouble. The cry or the shout cannot be voiced because it's almost literally being swallowed down. This can be seen by the movements of the Adam's apple. It's very difficult to work with this particular segment, because the patient is truly unaware that he's swallowing his rage or his grief, and also because we literally cannot get our hands on the larynx. What we can do is stimulate the gag reflex which moves counter to the swallowing and so may release the cry or shout. The gag reflex goes along with elevation of the diaphragm and with exhalation. You cannot cry or shout if you only inhale. But you can remain stiff-necked. When a patient complains to me of a stiff neck, I always look for withholding—what is he too proud to give in to? What is he hunched up against, for what is he holding himself in readiness? These are good areas in which to fantasize. I used to get stiff necks fairly often; I was too proud to ask for things I wanted—the "other" should of course know without being told. Ye gods! The demands we make! I discovered that if I rotated my head on my neck, down, around, up, down, around, up, and then in the opposite direction, I became all soft and relaxed and able to be taken care of. I sometimes use this exercise with a stiff-necked patient, and if they really allow themselves to get with it, the accompanying change in facial expression is remarkable. All the lines seem to change direction. It's a good time to ask them what they want. Even if it's only a massage.

We may move from the neck segment to the fourth—or chest—segment of the armor. The muscles which are involved in this segment are the intercostal muscles (those between the ribs), the pectoral or large chest muscles, the deltoid or shoulder muscles and the muscles on and between the shoulder blades. This armoring is expressed in an attitude of chronic inspiration, shallow breathing and immobility of the thorax. Inspiration, or holding one's breath, is a marvelous way to repress any emotion. What we are faced with then is self-control and restraint; the pulled back shoulders literally convey "pulling back" and repressed spite. Instead of the heart-breaking crying or raving

67

rage that one would expect from a mobile chest, one gets a cold rage. Crying is considered childish, longing implies softness and lack of character.

The arms and hands are extensions of the chest. Movements that are both giving and graceful stem from a mobile chest, whereas awkwardness, inaccessibility and distance result from the immobilization of this segment. It would be impossible to be a fluid, inspired dancer or a creative artist without chest mobility, just as it would be difficult to have true military carriage without immobility.

I had asked a man in one of my workshops to get up out of his chair, walk across the room and return to his chair. I then had someone imitate his walk so that he could see what it looked like. He felt that the imitation was exaggerated, that though he walked with pride, he did not walk with arrogance or hauteur, but the group insisted that that was how they saw him. They then tried to get him to wave his arms and jump up and down until he was out of breath, which he finally did. When he then walked across the room he was much looser and not nearly so formidable. Even the expression on his face had opened up.

Another odd symptom associated with the armoring of the chest, one which it is sometimes difficult to do away with, is the feeling of a "knot" in the chest similar to the one in the pharynx associated with *globus hystericus*. One way of dissolving the knot is to have the person lie supine on the floor and press in his chest while he yells at the same time. Reich feels it is particularly important to concentrate on the dissolution of the chest armor since it is in this specific segment that so many serious diseases originate: diseases of the heart, and diseases of the lungs such as emphysema and cancer. This area is also the source of giving and surrender.

The fifth armor segment is comprised of the diaphragm, stomach, solar plexus, pancreas and liver. In this segment it is more difficult than in the preceding four to translate the expressive language into word language. Possibly we could describe it with the word nausea. At any rate we know that the diaphragmatic armor may be dissolved with excessive expiration and gagging—up to and sometimes including the act of vomiting. While the armor is intact, the individual is unable to vomit and is almost constantly nauseous. We could perhaps assume that the person most prone to introjection suffers most from this kind of armoring—and from nervous stomach disorders.

I recall working with a young man once whose answer to life until that time had been, "no, no". He was unable to say yes to pleasure or yes to sharing, a kind of attitude which often accompanies immobility of the diaphragm. On the day in question he was especially unhappy and withdrawn. He complained of burning pains in his stomach, but he didn't think he was sick. I asked him to imagine himself very small and to go down into his stomach. With some reluctance he started the journey down through his mouth and past his tonsils, through the esophagus and into the stomach. There he encountered a fiery red ball so hot that he ran all the way up again. He said it was so hot that he couldn't explore it. I asked if there were any way to cool it off. He said, "Well, I could go back into my mouth and collect buckets of spit and see if that would do it." So he collected the buckets of spit and made the long journey down into his stomach again where he poured the spit over the fiery ball. It sputtered and sputtered and finally cooled off enough to touch, so he brought it up with him to show it to me. But it had turned an ashy black. Looking at it and looking at me he realized that this black ashy ball was his loneliness which he had been unable to share and even unable to explore on his own since it hurt so much. With the two of us sharing it he was not nearly so lonely, and the burning pains in his stomach disappeared.

One of the messages I'm trying to put across is that there is more than one way to deal with body armor. It's not always possible, for example, to make a person vomit up loneliness literally, but a fantasy will sometimes serve the same purpose.

The sixth armor ring is represented by a contraction in the middle of the abdomen. Reich says that "the spasm of the large abdominal muscles...goes with a spastic contraction of the lateral muscles which run from the lower ribs to the upper margin of the pelvis. They can be easily palpated as hard, painful cords" (Reich, 1949, p.388). The lower section of the muscles running along the spine, also felt as hard, painful cords, parallel this arrangement in the back. This segment of the armor is supposedly the easiest to dissolve but I have had little experience doing this. I would certainly imagine that the seat of intestinal disturbances would be found in this sixth segment, that patients with colitis would probably be helped by its increased mobility. This is something I have yet to discover.

The seventh segment is the pelvis. In most instances this segment is made up of almost all the muscles of the pelvis. The pelvis itself is retracted and sticks out in the back; it is dead and expressionless. Just as with the armoring of the shoulders, there is a specific pelvic anxiety and a specific pelvic rage. "Orgastic impotence creates *secondary* impulses to achieve sexual gratification by force" (Reich, 1949, p.389). What Reich is saying is that an individual who feels the beginnings of sexual excitement in such a way that he wants to give may then be blocked by his own pelvic armor so that the giving changes to rage. This is accompanied by violent forward movements of the pelvis which, if translated into words, would express anger and contempt for the sexual partner. After the dissolution of the pelvic armor, after the dissolution of the anxiety and the rage, the movement of the pelvis changes to a gently forward motion expressive of desire, of giving surrender, of longing.

I was working with a woman at one time and was having some difficulty locating the special thing about her which made her appear hard and aggressive. It was not her words particularly; I could use the same words and not sound aggressive. I finally asked her to walk for me, but was still puzzled. Her arms and shoulders were graceful and loose and her facial expression was

70

softly smiling, yet she still appeared aggressive. I tried imitating her walk myself and discovered that in order to capture its essence I had to keep my pelvis and hips very stiff. I told her this and suggested that she sway her hips slightly from side to side as she walked. She was reluctant because it might look sexy. I persuaded her anyway. She *did* look sexy and very *un*aggressive—and as she slowly became accustomed to her new gait she began to enjoy it immensely. Her skirts have become steadily shorter, and the impression she creates much warmer.

Underlying all seven segments of Reichian armor we have what Erving Polster calls the conveyor, the unifier, the source of support, namely, the breathing function. It would be almost worthless for us to mobilize any of the body segments if the proper kind of breathing did not accompany this process. One cannot shout on an inhalation, one cannot sigh on an inhalation; one can only imitate something that sounds like rales or at best a gasp.

When we hold our breath we tend to stop all movement, all emotion and, needless to say, almost all voice. In a sense we stop all being. How much more profitable it would be to breath, to move, to *be* freely—or at least with a freedom of choice.

71

4
FRAGMENTS OF GESTALT THEORY

Whenever I am asked to briefly discuss the subject of Gestalt theory, I think first of two things: the word "Gestalt" itself, and the concept of figure-ground. What is a Gestalt? It is a cohesive *one*. It derives from the German word "gestalten" which signifies form and means to *make a form* or a *comprehensive one*. If, for example, you think of a melody as a Gestalt, you become aware that any number of things may be done to it without changing its cohesive oneness; you may vary the key in which it is written, you may vary the rapidity with which it is played, you may play it loudly, softly or on a series of different instruments and yet retain unchanged the melodic line. It remains recognizable. So too does an individual. He may vary his mood, he may vary his responsiveness, his clothes or his words. He still remains John or Jeremy. There is more to a melody or a person than its various components—there is a wholeness.

It is important to remember that the way in which this Gestalt is perceived is a function of a figure-ground relationship and the direct result of the focus of attention. Let me try to make this more clear. All happenings, or perceptions, occur in a field with various elements shifting from foreground to background to make different forms or gestalten.

Say, for example, that I am talking to you. If the things I say to you are interesting or important, you will perceive me as figural and yourself as background. If on the other hand, you do not find me interesting or are preoccupied instead with what is going to happen to you when this workshop really starts rolling, your own feelings of discomfort and/or apprehension will become figural—in other words, attended to—and I or my voice or words will become background. Even my image may blur.

I can illustrate this phenomenon more graphically with a simple set of parallel lines. If you look at the lines in one way, you will see:

| | | | | |

which probably appear to you as five pairs of lines set a short distance apart from one another. The lines because of their proximity to one another are seen as figural upon a white background.

If I quickly add another series of lines, the figure becomes:

which then appears to be a series of four rectangles. As you can see, what was formerly figure has become ground, blank spaces between the series of rectangles. The incomplete rectangles at the ends of the rows may be completed in the mind's eye thru the principle of *praegnanz*—or becoming. The same sorts of changes in perception occur in human relationships.

The academic Gestalt psychologists never applied the principles of Gestalt formation, the principles of similarity, symmetry, proximity and praegnanz, to organic perceptions, namely, those perceptions which pertain to one's own feelings, emotion, or body awareness. Nor did they integrate the problems

74

of motivation with those of perception.[1] It remained for Frederick Perls to do so. By conceiving of the need-fulfillment pattern in the individual as a process of gestalt formation and destruction, he was able to make the role of perception, so useful to the academicians, available to the field of human behavior—always retaining as a critical element the factor of attention.

Let us go back to our musical example. Say that it is fairly late in the evening, that I have had dinner a number of hours ago and that I am sitting in a comfortable chair, in a softly lit room listening to Beethoven's Ninth, the third movement. The room, the chair, my own body are background. My felt need is for music and the music is figural. As I listen, however, I become aware of slight rumblings in my stomach and a feeling of emptiness. I ignore this and return to the music, but Beethoven has lost some of his savor; my attention becomes divided between my ear and my stomach and now a new phenomenon occurs—I suddenly see a vision—a jar of pickled herring unopened in the refrigerator. This is followed by a new sensation, my mouth begins to water and I can almost taste the onions on my tongue. Needless to say, Beethoven is quickly becoming background. I get up, walk into the kitchen, put some herring and a piece of rye bread on a plate and happily fall to. At this moment the food has become figural. Finished with it, I walk back into the living room where the Ode to Joy is now filling the house, sink happily back into my chair and allow the music again to fill my consciousness.

In Gestalt psychotherapy we describe this process as the progressive formation and destruction of perceptual and motor gestalten. As you can see, the need tends to organize both the perceptual qualities of the individual's experience and his motor behavior. In other words, the need energizes behavior and

---

[1] Fantz, like many Gestalt therapists at the time, seems to have been unaware of the later work of Kurt Goldstein and Kurt Lewin which focused on precisely these problems (Cf. discussion in Wheeler, 1991.) — Ed.

organizes it on the subjective-perceptual side and the objective-motor side.

Once we become aware of how this process works, we find ourselves possessed of an autonomous criterion of adjustment. We need no longer decide whether the individual is mature or immature by certain cultural standards. We need not decide whether the individual conforms to society. The important thing is that in the integrated person this process is always going on without interruption. New figures are constantly being formed; when the needs which organize their formation are satisfied, these figures are destroyed and replaced by new ones. But we must remember that unless the need is clear, it cannot energize the fruitful behavior necessary for biological or psychological survival.

Only as the individual can extract from his environment the things which he needs in order to survive, to feel comfortable, to be interested in the world around him, will he be able to live on a satisfactory biological level on the one hand and a satisfactory psychological level on the other. One cannot breathe without breathing in the environment; one generally cannot get affection without the knowledge that one wants it, or without the ability to communicate this want. This necessitates that the individual be sufficiently aggressive to interrupt his environment. In other words, he may be impolite and healthy or polite and neurotic.

It is good to know that there are clues available which tell us that all is going well in the formation and destruction of gestalten. For one thing, when this process is proceeding smoothly, the figure and ground become sharply differentiated; the individual knows what he wants; his field is not cluttered and only one thing draws his attention. For another, his motor behavior becomes well-organized, unified, coherent and directed toward the satisfaction of his need. The perceptual system and the motoric feed one into the other.

One of my most vivid memories of this kind of integrated behavior goes back to the time when my daughter, Lori, was first being toilet trained. At that time I had an office in my home and saw most of my patients there. Lori had learned very early that when my office door was closed she was not, under any circumstances, to come into the room, and up until that time she had never tried to do so. Bust she was also very involved with the idea of dry diapers and accomplishment. On this particular day she had finally used her potty successfully and was so enraptured of the idea and so motivated to tell me all about it immediately that she came running down the hall, banged wildly on my closed door and shouted again and again, "Mommy, Mommy, Lori made trickle in potty!" Obviously none of the "shoulds" had as yet forced her to repress her exuberance and spontaneity, nor to interrupt her need satisfactions.

All of us know, however, from our own experiences, that the smooth progression from formation to destruction of gestalten breaks down at times, often because the aforementioned shoulds get in the way. Again we are provided with clues which point up this failure. These clues can be seen both subjectively by the individual and objectively by the therapist or other interested observer. From the point of view of the subject there is confusion. He does not know what he wants; he does not know what is important; he cannot decide among alternatives. Since there is no sense of clarity, his attention is divided among fuzzy non-choices.

The observer on the other hand is presented with fixed and repetitive behavior. It's as if the subject were saying, "If at first you don't succeed, try the same thing again." The observer is also faced—or not faced—with lack of interest and effort, as if the subject were saying "nothing is really exciting; I have to force myself to do anything at all." Accompanying this perseveration and lack of affect is, understandably, a poor level of organization of both thought and speech.

Before we can deal constructively with the interferences that prevent need–fulfillment, we must examine what they are. We have found these interferences to be of three kinds. In the first place our subject is plagued by poor perceptual contact with the external world. That is to say, the space he inhabits, the people and things that he encounters incompletely, and the sounds, smells and sights which impinge on him from outside the self. At the same time (or at alternating times), the subject may maintain poor contact with his own body. A therapist may observe that the individual with whom he's working does not look at him directly nor at other significant portions of his immediate environment. He may not be aware of what he is doing with his hands, or of how his own voice sounds.

Because of this lack of awareness of both inner and outer stimuli, our subject is kept—or keeps himself—from encountering his own needs. If he does not encounter the need, he prevents himself in turn from giving any open expression to it. By failing to express it, he militates against its ever being satisfied. Obviously, if it does not get satisfied, it cannot get discharged but remains lurking somewhere in the person's global field, interfering with whatever other need might be able to organize the field in a clear-cut, coherent way.

One of the chief mechanisms for preventing the awareness of one's own needs is repression. Repression is seen by the Gestalt therapist as primarily a motor process, a muscular phenomenon. In order for a need to be expressed, some movement normally has to take place, either a gross body movement which moves an individual from one place to another or a fine, subtle movement which may only involve the twitch of an eyebrow. Any response—be it to the outside environment or to one's own inner climate—tends to play itself out on a motor level and can only be inhibited by contracting antagonistic muscles.

This can best be illustrated by using some phenomenon such as the need to get angry. When one thinks of anger, one envisions a frown, or the pulling down of the muscles of the mouth, clenched teeth, and the hand striking out in the urge to hit. But when anger, appropriate or otherwise, is somehow unacceptable to the person beginning to feel it, it is stopped by the smooth brow, the smiling mouth and the tightly clenched hands.

If this muscular response to an emerging feeling is indulged in habitually, the person using it eventually becomes quite unaware of his own original impulse. He ultimately becomes unaware as well of the grimace on his face which started out to be a smile. In this way all sorts of impulse unawarenesses are maintained by chronic muscular contractions which, in turn, have been forgotten by the individual using them.

Given the individual's poor perceptual contact with the external world and his own body, and given the individual's difficulty in allowing open expression of his own needs or even the ability to experience them because of chronic muscular contractions, where do we as therapists find ourselves? Happily, I can say that the Gestalt therapist works almost exclusively in the present. Instead of saying, as did the Freudians, "Where Id was, let Ego be," we are inclined to say, "I and Thou; Here and Now." Although the past is important in special circumstances, particularly when the individual is so stuck there that he cannot confront current realities, usually the therapist is able to work with what is immediately in front of him. He has the opportunity to see the confusions as they arise and so see what the person is doing to cause his own confusion. Even dreams and fantasies which were used chiefly as interpretive tools by the analysts may be used as guides to the subject's present life by dealing with the different facets of them as if they were the subject's own projections.

Much of the therapist's activity is directed to the breaking up of the individual's chronically poorly organized field. He does this by isolating portions of the field into smaller sub-units which better allow for direct attention. To do this he may employ what we sometimes call a shuttle technique, that is, a technique which permits the person to move from the event he is talking about to the pain in his own gut, to his fantasy about the therapist's motives, back to the feeling he may be having about himself at that particular moment in time.

As each new figure emerges, the therapist will attempt to heighten it, perhaps by having the subject exaggerate a movement which may accompany it, perhaps by examining the resistances which the subject affords himself. Let us say for example that the person looks sad, that his eyes are misty but that he never quite cries. The therapist may ask not "Why don't you cry?"—because very likely the person doesn't really know, but "How do you prevent yourself from crying?" In trying to answer this, the individual may discover that he's been holding his breath or that the muscles of his face are rigid from smiling. The object of this is not to take away the resistances of the resistor—he may still have a real need for them!—nor is it to destroy his ability to control his own behavior, but rather to make him aware of what he is doing so that he may choose what he does.

Finally, it must be remembered that just as the client is there with his frailties and hang-ups, so it is the therapist there with his. Both are there together as real human beings whose only live point of contact during that hour is the significant other. Initially, as in all human contact, there is a barrier, more or less permeable, which can only truly be bridged through feelings shared and emotions bared—not only by the client but by the therapist as well. Therapy is not a one-way street.

PART II : REFLECTIONS

5
BEGINNINGS

How to start.

Where to start.

In all my years of practice I've developed no set way.

One of the things my original sessions have in common is that I go into the lobby where a new client is waiting—or not, depending on his timing—and I introduce myself with the hope that I've picked the right face to go with my fantasy. Occasionally I guess wrong.

Actually, my first session as I know it does not begin with the arrival of the client on the scene. Rather, it starts with a series of telephone calls in one of which the prospective client and I finally get to talk to one another. During that conversation I usually collect some statistical data: age, marital status, type of employment, referral source and presenting problem. I also try to find out if they're covered by some type of insurance since my fees are high, and it's important that they feel they can pay them or that I can adjust if they can't.

At this point in time I'm particularly interested in their referral source since many people know me well enough to send me clients I can work with well—usually a good prognosticator— and some don't know me at all and may make a definite mismatch.

If both the prospective client and I like the sound of each other, and if our schedules can be made to mesh, we set up an appointment time. Often by the time this is done we both kind of have a feel for one another—frequently relatively accurate, occasionally dead wrong.

I realize that many of you are working in agencies where your clients are assigned to you and that often the person who does the intake (and on whom the client may frequently become imprinted) is not the same man or woman who ends up doing the therapy or the crisis intervention—which of course may present problems. What you may have to deal with in your initial session is the very real difference between the original interviewer and yourself. What were your client's expectations and how do you coincide with them? How do you differ? These are questions to be explored early on or the therapy may never get off the ground. Is it possible to capitalize on your differences if they are a source of client resistance? Is there a way that they can be used to advantage? A captive client needs to be seduced into consent rather than compliance or you have a lost cause on your hands.

For example, if Mary Ann is expecting to work with a man, because she's always gotten along better with men than women, and she feels most of her problems originated with her mother—first you need to discover whether it's possible to persuade her that she now has an excellent opportunity to work with a woman—unlike her mother—from whom she may receive some of the support and acknowledgment that she never got previously. Or you might let her know that working with a man, no matter how originally pleasant or comfortable, is merely repeating a pattern she's indulged in many times before without solving any of her underlying difficulties.

I'm aware even as I say this that what I'm talking about is the captive client—with one who can pick and choose, a hard sell—or even a soft one—may be a real turn-off. Particularly with the client who is "shopping around." I'm thinking specifically of a young man who I saw initially several weeks ago. He had been in analysis for several years, and though he had made some progress, he felt that he could go no further in that particular milieu. He

BEGINNINGS

had consequently interviewed a therapist in T.A., one in RET and finally me for gestalt.

This was a session in which I essentially got interviewed rather than the client; he wanted to know whether I had the expertise to get him through his obsessional phase, and how I would go about it. God knows *I* didn't know whether I could indeed get him past his self-torment, but I did have an idea of *how* I might go about getting him to work on it—and this I did share with him. It wasn't until he asked me point blank what my credentials were that I spelled them out for him. At no point did I promise that "our" way would "cure" him. He subsequently indicated that had I done so, he would have gone to someone else. As it was it took him three weeks to arrive at a decision to work with me. I was surprised that he did.

Unless I'm asked, I do not normally lay out a course of therapy in an initial session. In the first place, I do not as yet know the client well enough to design a course of therapy; in the second, I like to work very much in the here and now—from moment to moment. Designing a course of therapy for me is akin to pigeonholing my client. I am almost forcing myself to hold to my original impression so I may stick to my design—thus freezing Jane or Jerry in a mode from which it is difficult for them to move.

Almost always a client enters my office for the first time with no idea of where to start. He may know he's hurting, he may not, but he's so bombarded with internal stimuli that he's either unable to verbalize or trying to get everything out in one breath.

There's a temptation to say, "well, begin at the beginning; tell me about your family, your childhood, your education." I resist this. I know there are those who don't; we all have our individual styles—and often during intakes in agencies, these are precisely the questions that are dealt.

But my sense is that when I follow that route, I end up with an abundance of "talking about" which can set the tone for future sessions. So I usually try to get my client comfortable and

85

centered, and ask her to take her time and look around and start with the first thing that comes to mind—whatever is foreground for her.

Now, clients differ widely in that which is foreground for them. Clearly, awareness may be directed toward the outside—namely the persons or objects in the environment—or toward the self; toward that which is affective—for example, emotions and feelings—or that which is cognitive—intuitions, visualizations, thoughts, memories, wishes, metaphors, fantasies, dreams.

What is originally figural for your client may be a very good clue as to who he is, what makes him tick and where his resistances may lie. For example, if someone walks into my office on a bright blue sunny day, pays no attention to the look of the room or me in it, slumps on my love seat, looks down at his navel and immediately starts talking about the guilt he has surrounding his obsessive thoughts, I know I'm in for a long, trying course of therapy—one that will involve a lot of body work and a lot of undoing of retroflections, God preserve me from saying so. This is one of the times I may choose to disguise my authenticity.

I remember many years ago when I was very new to therapy and very attuned to Perls and consequently laid out all the things I was thinking to just such a client. My feeling was that I was doing a brilliant job. He was fascinated with me. He never came back.

If on the other hand, someone walks into my office on the same kind of blue day, remarks on the loveliness of the snow leaning on the window, says how fine it must be to work in such a surround, I know either that I'm dealing with someone who has a sense of otherness as well as self—who is at least partially attuned to what is—or is adept at hiding her innermost feelings, or both. But I have a vehicle with which to work—a starting place: How do her insides compare to the day? If they match, what is she doing here? If they don't, is the difference painful? Either way, we quickly get to a pertinent part of herself; we tap into energy.

We also tap into what she wants from me—a possible place to establish a contract. It goes without saying (but if I remember, I say it anyway) that out primary focus is always on the client: his needs, his wants, his blind spots, his resistances. I am there to listen, to encourage, to facilitate, to develop a floor of support, to confront those things he is unable to confront himself. I share myself, my thoughts, my feelings when they are pertinent to what he is experiencing or *could* be experiencing—but not when they are deflective and make me the focus.

Of course, when a client enters my office and immediately begins to cry, I have no time to establish a contract. When a client enters my office on the verge of hysterics, I have no time to establish a contract. Instead, I get out the box of Kleenex, place it within reach and make myself available for any outpourings that are about to emerge. This is usually a time for silence on my part, or reassurance that the tears which are quickly subsiding need more of a chance to come out. It's a time to establish that crying is permissible, in fact necessary, and that everyone who *can* cries here.

So many of my clients are initially ashamed of their tears or their anger or their theatrics; it is up to me – it is up to you—to let them know that our office is a safe place to indulge them, experiment with them so that they may grow into their many sidedness. It is a place to let them know that we take them very seriously – but sometimes with a soupcon of humor.

It is not a place to be confluent, at least totally so, even during a first session. I remember some years back, when a new client was telling me some horrendous tale of her daily life, and laughing incongruently at the same time. In my naivete I laughed too, and was immediately castigated for my lack of feeling and perception. She was quite right. I've long ago learned that her laughter was a deflection from her pain, and I was abetting her in that deflection. There's a definitive line between support and confluence.

What to *do* in an initial session? Establish an ambience where your client feels safe, where she feels heard, where she becomes aware that you don't con easily. Simple enough to say – somewhat harder to do. Because no two people can do it in the same way. Because no two people are the same people. It's essential that you establish your own base for comfort, for groundedness – whether that means sitting quietly in a chair or strolling around your office. It's essential that you know who you are, which of your actions are authentic – expressive of you and not a reasonable facsimile – which of your actions are a deliberate disguise that is necessary at that moment for the benefit of your client. For example, not interrupting a gushing flow of words that needs to come out even though you have to bite your tongue to stop yourself. But later giving yourself the chance to tell your client how it felt for you to do this and your motivation for allowing him to continue.

The one thing that I do that is always the same in an opening session is the ending of it. I never assume that my client and I will continue to work together. I always ask how the hour went for them, what they might or might not have learned, and how they feel about working with me, Sometimes they don't know; they need time to think it over. Sometimes, they're flying high and want to come back the next day. But usually they've profited from where we've been, they experience me as someone they can trust and talk to and are willing to set up weekly appointments. If I feel the same way, we do.

I do not always know how it is for you to carry back to places where you work the notions that many of us espouse here at the Institute. I'm sure they're sometimes useful and a turn-on and sometimes so strange to the people you work with that they create for you nothing but trouble. It's important to weave them into the things you do outside of here so that you can create for yourself a rich and vibrant fabric that doesn't induce others to cut your threads—to perhaps in some creative way weave their ideas into the fabric too. If we can help, we will.

6
WORKING IN THE NOW

Working in the now—a now unattached to past or future—is how many of the uninitiated and, unfortunately, some of the initiate as well, regard the work of the Gestalt therapist. I have myself on occasion said "I and thou, here and now." But when I say this, I do not mean to imply that this "here" and this "now" is comprised merely of momentary fragments, fireflies that flicker and fade. That way lies psychopathy, instant gratification, lack of conscience or existential guilt.

My "here" and my "now"—and I trust yours, as well—is linked with chains of steel, chains of gossamer, chains of darkness and light not only to my past but to my future as well. Each minute segment of our present awareness has been shaped from the fabric of our history and the less substantial material of our future wants and wishes. These, in turn, have been shaped from our history, the individuals who have had impact on our lives, and the apperceptive mass comprised of all things read, heard, seen and felt in the process of moving from then to now. The moments of the now are *heavy* moments laden, often unaware, with both what has been and what is to be.

Anyone who believes that dealing solely with these present moments without verifying what has led to them and where in turn they may lead might as well believe in the so-called "black box" of the Skinnerian. It is certainly true that contact is made in the present; but the *kind* of contact made—its potency and duration—is a factor not only of the therapist's knowledge of and skill in using the rules of contact, but of the availability of the client to be present. This availability, or lack thereof, is a product of all that has gone before as well as what is occurring in the moment—not only for the client but for the therapist as well.

Most of us wear masks. The client does because he needs to develop trust before he can allow himself to be seen. The therapist, particularly the novice (but the trained practitioner too) wears them because he also does not wish to be seen as other than skillful and professional—certainly not vulnerable. And the masks we wear are the products of fixed perceptual frameworks, fixed ways in which we view the world. They derive in part from a discipline we've immersed ourselves in—the supervisors who demand a particular stance, and our own value system.

Now the ways in which we view the world are expressed in the themes we bring into a therapy session, and these themes in turn represent the stories we tell ourselves. They are the best stories we can devise for what brought us to this moment of time—this heavy moment.

Certainly there are many instances when our themes represent us and our histories truly, and when this is so, therapy can proceed smoothly from uppermost figure (which includes a need/want and a resistance to that need/want, plus a direction) to experiment—which is a culmination of a major portion of work. But there are also many instances when our themes have evolved through distortions, where our awareness of self and other is shaped not by accurate perceptions but by introjections and projections such as: 1) one must never question authority, 2) one must always be happy; 3) you are judgmental, 4) you are jealous. Our "now" may preclude total awareness because of what has caused it to be misshapen or rubbed to a glowing patina to blind us to the flaws in the structure.

Consider for a moment. A client comes into therapy because his defenses—his armor in our terms—are crumbling, and he is afraid. If he's able to say this, rather than wear the mask of fearlessness, and indicate that he would like to 1) re-establish his armor, or 2) learn to live in a way that would not necessitate so thick a bounding, or 3) learn what he needs to defend *against*,—

then we have no problem (if we're in good shape ourselves.) But suppose our client is *unable* to explore any of these directions—either of his or our own instigation—because he had introjected the notion that fear is bad, is to be deplored or will cause his world to crumble, as it *is* crumbling and has crumbled before. Suppose he has seen his father afraid, depressed, taken to hospital—none of which we know in this moment of time—what then do we do to maximize this moment? Certainly we do not jump in with both feet using all the esoteric skills we have honed in the past few years, which might well result in our client (rightly) regarding us as some strange species of human or beast as he makes a mad dash for the door. Nor do we sit silently in our chairs, face impassive, mask in place, assuming that this new individual will magically—and without training—present us with an uppermost figure. Forget it. He or she is scared to death.

If you can bracket off for a few seconds that you too are a touch frightened given that you are entering into a largely unknown situation, you might attempt to recapture some of the feelings you, yourself, experienced when you first saw your initial therapist, or your second, or perhaps even your third. Did he sit silently and allow you to flounder? Did she bombard you with questions that felt totally irrelevant at the time? Did he have you lie on a couch and direct you to free associate while taking notes behind your back? Or did she hopefully—and with some modicum of grace—put you at ease?

Can you recall your initial discomfort, your wonder as to why you had come to this strange place at all? Did you assume that this unknown individual sitting across from you, or behind you, or next to you could analyze you and categorize you without your ever saying a word—that, in effect, he could read your mind and judge you to boot?

Chances are good that your new client is feeling the same way and thinking some of the same thoughts. In addition he/she is probably regarding himself as some sort of guinea pig who is exposing himself not only to you but to your (and his) observers

91

as well. Hardly a situation that evokes ease, comfort and trust. Now if your perceptual framework calls for you to be cool, aloof, apparently all knowing, inasmuch as this view is the introject you have lived with regarding "therapists," you are in an untenable position for putting your client at ease. I've been working with a couple for the past few months where the wife is seeing another therapist in individual therapy. Her constant complaint is that she always leaves her sessions in worse shape than she came in because her therapist never answers a question, never starts a session, makes cryptic interpretations and sees her once a week. If one is doing psychoanalysis four or five times a week this sort of approach could be workable; on a once a week basis it appears to be a disaster. But clearly her therapist is wearing the cool, aloof, all-knowing mask. I do not know if she is feeling insecure; I only know she is ineffective. Needless to say, I do not recommend such an attitude to you.

Nor do I recommend that you instantly tell your client how uncomfortable you, too, are. Again, your client would start wondering what on earth she is doing here with you. You are supposed to (*and do*) know something! I recommend that you be real—authentically you, attuned not only to the look and sound and kinesthetic "feel" of your client but to your own proprioceptions as well—the sensations and awareness of your gut, your heart and your head.

Bear in mind that your own unfinished business, your own frame of reference, those pieces of your own past history that remain unresolved affect the way in which you apperceive your client—just as your client's frame of reference affects how he sees you. If, for example, you have had a good relationship with your mother, working with a woman older than yourself may be rewarding and delightful (unless, of course, you are meeting someone totally unlike the mother you knew). If, on the contrary, your mother was a fount of punishment, of jealousy, of guilt trips, working with an older woman could prove a source of pitfalls and constant alert discomfiture. As therapists we too have our countertransferences and our projections. Difficult though it may be to set them aside temporarily, it is imperative that we do so. Incumbent upon us is the awareness that we are setting them aside, which does not mean they cease to exist but that we must be vigilant in not permitting them to interfere and make of the moment something it need not be. Say to yourself what you might at some point direct a client to say: "This is *not* my mother; how is she different? How is she similar? Let me count the ways."

Let's return to the client who walks into our office because his defenses are crumbling, his armor is coming unhinged, and he is afraid. All this he knows, but he is wearing the mask of intrepidity and insouciance to prevent us from knowing, in spite of the reality that he needs (though perhaps doesn't want) our help in coming to terms with where he is. A dilemma.

Where to begin? Where to approach this present moment so as to crystallize its meaning? A frequent approach is giving in to our curiosity. Most of us are curious about human behavior or we would never have become therapists in the first place; a therapist devoid of curiosity does not belong in the field. And most of us are interested in the client sitting in the other chair. To hide this interest is nonsense; whether one is afraid or shy or hiding, one still warms to another's interest. But at the same time, one may flee from it. It's important to be aware of both these possibilities as you makes your initial foray. After an opening remark or greeting it is always appropriate to ask, "And what brings you to talk to me at this particular time?" Granted, you may not expect a direct answer, and our crumbling client is unlikely to give you one. He may instead shunt you off and deflect with a remark about the weather or the thickness of the snow outside the window or how comfortable he finds himself in your chair. If you pay attention to the phenomenological data as well as his words, you may notice that as he speaks of the comfort of the chair, his hands are gripping the arms of it as though he might never let go. A first or second session is too soon to point out the discrepancy between his words and his posture, but it is not too soon to remark that he sounds remarkably self-possessed and that you wonder what he might hope to get from any therapeutic intervention. And it's true; you do wonder this. As a matter of fact, so does he. But if he says "nothing," he puts himself in the position of looking the fool—an intolerable place to be—and if he says "something," he is obligated, in his own eyes at least, to give you some clue as to what has brought him here originally. At this point what you do is critical. Sitting back in your chair and intoning, "hmmm," could turn him off forever or at best move him back into his armored position. Leaning forward and evincing interest with or without words is a step in the right direction. Voicing the notion that though he appears comfortable, it must be a difficult feeling to maintain in a new and strange situation, *could* give him the sense that you are possessed of empathy; and continuing with the statement that in his place you might find yourself at a loss might give him an additional sense of who you are and present an opening wedge for some burgeoning of trust.

Some sense of trust. Total trust is a long time coming and attempting to push for it with blatantly false and premature reassurances is less than useful. Your client needs a testing time, perhaps a pushing of the limits as does the small child who wonders how far he can go without forcefully encountering your boundaries. He needs to know that although your tolerance is high (and that you will accept as true that which does not ring patently false), you can and *will* confront that which contradicts something said previously or behavior which appears obviously incongruent.

I find it truly amazing how time and again my allowing to slip out some small personal thing about myself—some sharing when it does not detract from what is being presented at the moment—can not only enrich the interaction but further the revelation or disclosure of the other. In the instance of our crumbling man my sharing that it was once eminently important to me to appear on top of any situation, but that it became too cumbersome to maintain that stance, permitted him to share the knowledge that his confident persona served to keep people at a distance—a distance that prevented them from distinguishing his frailty. Or from offering the help and succor which he could not—would not—accept in any but subtle and indirect ways.

It was in just such a way that he "told" me how I must act with him; I must never give overwhelmingly; I must never touch him physically or psychologically in other than artful, almost imperceptible ways; I must be crafty. And above all I must allow *him* to approach *me*. All difficult things for me to do—but imperative. This sharing of myself with my client, this bringing of my past into the present moment without the explicit demand that he do the same, is one way of planting seeds for future trust.

If it is possible for me to share, it may just be plausible that he could do the same. If I can present myself as unafraid, though less than perfect, I make it feasible for him to be imperfect as well. I make it feasible for him to present his crumbling facade without the fear that either he or I will disintegrate totally. When I indicate indirectly that who I am is a product in part of who I was, he can confront the possibility that his frightening past which has brought him to his perilous present can move him beyond the now to a more openly vulnerable but solid future. That hope for a solid future becomes a part of our present moment of time—our now.

I can perhaps more simply illustrate working in the moment—past, present, future—by relating a small piece of a therapy session that occurred just before Valentine's Day. My client, a young and attractive woman, was having some difficulty describing to me the valentine she had bought for her husband. She was dissatisfied with the valentine because it did not say what *she* wanted to say, but she was also dissatisfied with the relationship and unwilling to say to him more than she felt at any particular moment. I could certainly understand her difficulty, but was reluctant to leave her with her dissatisfaction. So moving

95

with my need I asked her if she would be willing to fantasize the perfect valentine, one that could express exactly what she wanted it to. She was silent for almost a minute, and then an expression of acute surprise showed on her face.

I mentioned that she looked startled and wondered what had happened in her fantasy. She replied that it was the strangest thing, but she had suddenly visualized a treasure chest! I asked her to open it and look inside. When she did she was amazed and very moved to discover the trove of gifts within. As her eyes misted over she recollected all the intangible gifts her husband had given her through the years: gifts of love, of support, of understanding. In that moment of time she realized how very much more he meant to her than she had surmised.

She was overwhelmed with her sudden love of him, and aware that the valentine she must now create had to convey so many things that that small moment of time—that "now" comprised of past, present, future—had brought into awareness.

7

POLARITIES

One of the areas that lends itself with great richness to the therapist who enjoys setting up experiments is that of polarities. I find it extremely interesting that in four books written wholly or in part by Frederick Perls there is no notation in the indices which pertains to this concept. And yet it is a concept which permeated much of his working style and which contributed heavily to his theories about dreams.

Of course, the concept and use of polarities did not originate with Perls, although he placed great emphasis on it. The opposites of Good and Evil, of God and the Devil, were certainly prevalent in the Christian bible as were the antitheses of yin and yang in Taoist thought. In psychology I encountered polarities first in my reading of Jung—primarily in his presentation of the archetypes. If you recall, Jung described his archetypes as the structural components of the collective unconscious, a universal thought form or idea which contains large elements of emotion. Among these archetypes he described the eternal compassionate mother as opposed to the devouring witch, birth as opposed to death, the hero contrasted with the child, and God as antagonistic to the Devil. And he posited that all these characters existed within us as more or less well-delineated facets of our personality. Jung stressed that the basic aspects of the psyche which the person has denied in his conscious living tend to exist and grow in the unconscious—as a shadow tends to reflect the mass of the real thing. For example, the person who typically thinks without feeling casts a long shadow in the feeling area. Because it is kept unconscious, Jung felt that the feeling area of such a person tends to remain primitive—and could grow to monstrous proportions. Therefore any eruption of feeling would tend to be experienced as fearful.

Jung believed that personality contains polar tendencies. He maintained that a psychological theory of personality must be founded on the principle of opposition or conflict because the tensions created by conflicting elements are the very essence of life. Without tension he felt there would be no energy and therefore no personality. Nor did he believe that the contest between rational and irrational forces of the psyche ever ceased.

It is important to remember that polar elements not only oppose one another, they also attract and seek one another, and that a balanced and integrated personality can only result through a synthesis of these polar traits. Now whether or not Perls' ideas about polarities derived from those of Jung, both men stressed the same principle, namely differentiation and integration. As Perls describes it, "The basic philosophy of Gestalt Therapy is that of nature—differentiation and integration. Differentiation by itself leads to polarities. As dualities, those polarities will easily fight and paralyze one another. By integrating opposite traits, we make the person whole again." (Perls, 1965, p.8)

Now Perls' favorite technique for getting at these opposing traits was the Top-Dog, Under-Dog experiment. He equated the Top-Dog essentially with the super-ego and characterized it as the autocrat or dictator—the part of the self which judges and tells one what to do. The Top-Dog is always righteous, has the right to criticize, to nag, to put one on the defensive. Yet in spite of the Top-Dog's apparent power, Perls felt that the Under-Dog always won out—usually through sabotage, evasion and postponement, just as do the masses under the heel of the dictator. But the winning was basically a negative thing since the person merely succeeded in stopping himself from doing what one part of him wanted to do. Perls felt that the solution could be found in a dialogue between the two selves (represented by the Top-Dog and the Under-Dog)—a dialogue that could lead to integration.

Interestingly when the two parts of the self start talking, it's almost always the case that—at first—neither side listens. One possible reason for this is that one dog or the other is often an introject which the individual has neither fully incorporated nor spit out. Not so oddly, then, the person is often unaware that there is someone else living in his skin. In a recent workshop, there was a very attractive young divorcee who wanted to get married again, but who discovered that she was unable to do so because the moment she became really important to a man, she not only lost interest in him but started treating him like dirt. She found this terribly upsetting but was apparently impotent to do anything about it. Now it was obvious that there were two parts to this woman in conflict, and my theory was that the lonely "wanting a man" self was essentially valid but that there was a highly potent top-dog that was somehow sabotaging her moves toward union. So I asked her to engage in a dialogue with herself which, after some demurring, she proceeded to do.

U.D.: I'm so lonely, I wish I had someone to come home to at the end of the day.

T.D.: You have the children; that should certainly be enough for you.

U.D.: I'm all right during the day as long as I'm busy, and at night I'm all right if I'm tired enough, but—

T.D.: Don't be such a baby; you should certainly be more self-sufficient than that!

U.D.: But I don't want to be self-sufficient! I want a man to take care of me, and make some decisions for me, and—

T.D.: Decisions, ha! What man is really strong enough to make your decisions? They're all weak—you'll end up taking care of him!

U.D.: I won't! Paul was wonderful about decisions, he made everything so easy for me, I really loved him until—

T.D.: Yah, until! Until he couldn't make a move without you, until you could do nothing except worry about his falling apart. You aren't any good for a man.

U.D.: But I want to be! I hate myself when I turn on men this way, when I can't give them the time of day after they've been so wonderful.

T.D.: Forget it baby, go it alone; you can do it, there's something wrong with all of them!

By this time my client was practically in tears and it was evident that her Top-Dog, Under-Dog dialogue had tapped some other source of pain. I asked her who her Top-Dog reminded her of and she said that it was her father who had treated her like a princess, had taken her out instead of her mother, had taken her to concerts and opera and who had planned to take her to see the world. Instead he'd died in agony in her arms.

So I had her change the experiment and play her father in dialogue with herself. This part was fun. Because once her father was outside of her she was able to see him as the loving but very clever man who with great finesse managed to sabotage every relationship she entered into. She did a beautiful job imitating his deprecating attitude toward her boyfriends, his building up of her ego, and his fostering of her dependency on himself. She was also able to see how she played along with this, because in essence he gave everything she wanted—except sex which, while he was still alive, she hadn't acknowledged as important. In addition, she became aware in the course of the experiment that she *still kept him alive* inside of her where he (as her Top-Dog) was desperately interfering with her life. It was time for her to say goodbye.

But she could not do this by herself. She could only dissolve in tears. So I once again changed the experiment and had one of the men in the group play her father, which he did with great skill. He was able somehow to convey all the wants of the father, his desire never to be supplanted, his need to go on living in her, without in any way removing from her the necessity of making a decision in regard to him. She in turn was able to say that she still loved him, that he had been very important to her but that he no longer really gave her anything. She could say that her only choice was to keep him alive and never have anyone else or allow him to die so that she could discover someone who in some way could meet and join her fully—if not as he had, at least with some measure of fulfillment. And she finally did choose to say goodbye.

Now the experiments I just cited point up several things quite clearly. The Top-Dog, Under-Dog polarity illustrates how two parts of the personality can emerge with some vividness. It also illustrates the fairly easy-to-detect presence of an introject. Finally, it shows how an introject, once recognized, can be dealt with and either digested or spit up. It is well to remember—and I cannot stress this too strongly—that it is difficult, if not impossible, to give up something which you do not know is there.

I find it quite fascinating that so often in the Top-Dog, Under-Dog experiments one finds an introject as representative of one of the Dogs. These introjects, however, need not always be spit out; sometimes it is incumbent on one to thoroughly digest them so as to liberate the locked up energy. An excellent demonstration of this occurred in another workshop I conducted somewhat earlier.

One of the young women in the group was a very pretty, sweet-looking youngster who consistently sat just outside the circle of events. Occasionally she appeared on the verge of tears but practically never said anything unless asked directly—and then her input was brief. On the last day of the workshop, fearing that she would leave more depressed than she was when she came in, I tried to get with how she was feeling. She was feeling miserable. She was angry and unable to vent her anger; she wanted to scream and couldn't allow herself to scream. She had spent three days being very nice to very nice people, when all she wanted to do was rail at them loudly and, failing this, go hide in her room.

Again I had her start with Top-Dog, Under-Dog dialogue and play her "nice" self against her "bitchy" self.

> U.D.: What makes you so nasty all the time? I don't even like the sound of you.

> T.D.: I hate nice people; I just want to strike out at them, tear them limb from limb.

> U.D.: You're shitty when you're like that. I don't see how anyone can stand you! Why don't you go hide away 'til you're bearable?

> T.D.: Talk about bearable! Wow! Do you put on an act—sugar wouldn't melt—who do you think you're fooling?

> U.D.: There you go again—always claiming to see right through me. Man, I need you like a hole in the head. At least people like me!

> T.D.: Like you! They don't even know you! At least I'm real even if I'm miserable. All you do is smile or cower in corners. No guts!

> U.D.: Oh, you have guts all right! But where would you be without me? Alone, that's where! No one could

stand you for two minutes! I can't stand you. I hate you!

By this time both dogs were screaming at one another, and it rather looked as if they could continue to do so for some time to come. So I asked Janey who she really wanted to scream at. And she screamed at me, "My mother! She's terrible—you can't believe how terrible, oh, I can't stand her, I can't stand her, I can't stand her!" At which point she buried her face in her hands and shuddered. It was obviously time for the dialogue with mama, so we switched to that, Jane playing both parts.

> Mama: Jane, you'd better go speak to your math teacher tomorrow, or you'll never get an A in that course.
>
> Jane: I don't care about the A, Mom. I'm doing fine.
>
> Mama: *(Whiny voice)* How can you say you're doing fine? All you want to seem to do is have fun! After I worked and slaved to send you to school. And what school do you choose? A silly little college in Indiana instead of all the good places you could go. With trash!
>
> Jane: Mama, I'm not coming home this summer, I don't want to drown this summer at home with you.
>
> Mama: But I expect you at home, everyone expects you home, everyone expects you home. Why, I've sewed three new dresses, and I want everyone to see you in them.
>
> Jane: I don't want the dresses! I want to do things for myself. I hate you taking care of me. Ever

since I was little you wanted to live my life for me.

Mama: I want you to live up to your potential, I want you to do the things I didn't do, have the things I didn't have. You're all I have! I want you to be a lady!

Jane: That's all you ever say! Mind you manners! Mind your grammar! Mix with the right people. Be sweet, be nice, I could die of it!

Here, she turned to me and said, "You're so sweet! How can you be so sweet? I don't understand it!" Whereupon my co-leader said cleverly, "Jane, you be Rennie, and Rennie, you do Jane." So, sort of blinkingly, we switched.

Me: Good grief, you're sweet! Ugh.

Jane: Well, it's easy when you understand everyone.

Me: Understand! You just sit there and absorb—with that kind look on your face. It turns my stomach.

Jane: *(smiles and nods her head)*

Me: My God, you sit there like some damned powder puff with no guts. I could just blow you away.

Jane: I'm not really a powder puff, I'm—

Me: So okay, not a powder puff, a pillow maybe, one you can pound and pound and it always goes back into shape! I'm so tired of pounding on you.

Jane: You could always stop.

Me: I won't stop! I'll make you budge somehow. You're killing yourself! You're sitting there damping all your fire and vitality; you're making yourself into a nothing, a shadow, and if you keep it up, you'll die!

Jane: Are you still me, or are you you now?

Me: I'm both. I'm the part of you that can't tolerate being stifled, I'm the part of you that's fighting for your life. I'm your power that's bubbling up and being quashed by your mama in you. But I'm also myself, myself who believes all the things I'm saying to you.

Jane: I like that, I like you when you talk like that. Maybe I could like myself if I could do it too.

So, perhaps we had got through an impasse. You may have noticed, though, that the pathway was at no point particularly straightforward. At first, we had the polarities of "nice" versus "bitchy," but it was quite unclear what generated either the niceness or the bitchiness. Gradually, with the shift to mama (who incidentally was not quite the kind of "terrible mom" I would have expected from Jane's tremendous rage with her) we discover that the bitchiness comes from mama but is disguised as "caring." But also from mama comes the introject of "nice" which mama, the super-ego, has demanded of Jane for years. So we have two introjects, both acquired from mama, and both impossible to digest since she cannot stand mama, nor allow herself to be in any way like her. Consequently, she cuts herself off from her own power by cutting herself off from her own aggression. Happily—in this instance—she could identify with my bitchiness and possibly allow herself the prerogative of using it since she had enjoyed it in me. If she becomes able to do this, she may also end up enjoying her own niceness.

Needless to say, experiments with opposites do not always work out so neatly. Just a week or so ago, I was seeing a fairly new client in therapy and trying to get some kind of a fix on the aggression which he took great pains to keep under wraps. He had an almost constant tremor in his right hand which two neurologists had labeled psychological and due to tension, but I had no clear idea of what the tension was about. On this particular day he had related to me a dream which was largely a melange of color. In it he was aware of a blob of red-orange which he could only conceptualize as Aquarius—Aquarius being the zodiacal sign of his beloved. Next to it was a blackish snake-like form which he identified as Scorpio and, to finish off the triumvirate, a red crab-shaped form which he interpreted as Cancer, his own astrological sign.

Unwilling to get caught up in all the symbolism the dream presented, I asked him to describe himself as the different parts of the dream and to start with the snake-like-form. He began, "I am the personification of evil. I am out to get you, Mary, (the red-orange blob) and to bend you to my will. I will drag you in the dirt and then cast you from me." All of which was said in a low, level voice with little expression. I remarked about the incongruence of his words and his feeling tone and asked him if he could make himself sound more evil and more gleeful. Which, to my surprise, he proceeded to do. "I will use you for my own satisfactions; I will degrade you and revile you and then grind you in the dust! There is nothing you can do to resist me! I will besmirch you, defile you and then toss you aside." His tone throughout this second attempt had become more and more unctuous, his expression had become more gloating, and he had started to rub his hands together in satisfaction; his tremor had all but disappeared. I applauded his characterization and then asked him to be the red crab.

He again began in a somewhat droning sing-song, "Never fear, fair maiden, I will rescue you! I am your knight in shining armor and I and my trusty steed will ride to your defense. I will

slay the villainous dragon and restore you to honor and chastity."
I remarked that he certainly sounded peaceful for someone about
to go into battle, to say nothing of sounding dull. He explained to
me that he was having all kinds of trouble (indeed, his hand was
trembling again) and that although he could think about going into
battle and even consider having won, he could not get with the
actual battle at all. So I said, "Fine, why don't you really try to do
that? Be both the evil serpent and the stalwart knight and have a
dialogue one with the other." He made several abortive attempts
to do so, all the time getting tighter and less and less real. When I
commented on this, he looked particularly troubled and began to
stammer. "I can't do it, I just can't do it; I'm getting more and
more panicky!" In truth he appeared quite upset, and I asked him
what he was afraid might happen. He responded, "I don't know—I
just feel as if I'll explode, as if something in my head would just
burst, and I'll, I'll—" "As if you'll flip your lid?" I asked. He sort
of nodded and I was quiet for a minute with fantasies of broken
crab shell all over the room, shining armor (note the analogy)
falling in shards and a possible triumphant serpent. But I didn't
push it. A part of me respected his very real fright, and I
withdrew. Nevertheless I did share with him, a little later, my
feeling that all his vitality and power were bound up in what he
considered the evil part of himself and that we would have to
search out constructive ways to let it emerge.

As you can see, we arrived at no simple denouement. We
never got around to working with the third part of the self—the
part openly vulnerable to attack—and we even ended the session
on a distinct note of uneasiness. Still, I have received no
frightened phone calls in the middle of the night as is sometimes
his wont, and I have a somewhat clearer picture as to where to
move. Needless to say, I also have a hodgepodge of symbolic and
metaphorical material which I can, if I choose, use in different
sorts of experiments.

Which brings me in a somewhat roundabout way to what
Perls talked about as integration. He stated that in psychotherapy

we look for the urgency of unfinished—or perhaps even undeveloped—situations in the present situation. And by present experimentation with new attitudes and new materials, we aim at new unities. It is not that the patient "remembers" himself as the Freudians might posit, but rather that he discovers and shapes himself.

As I have indicated, the resisting part of the personality has vitality and strength and often many other estimable qualities which are mired down in a host of introjects. Although it may take a long time and much energy to form a complete whole out of the fragmented parts of the personality, to fail to do so would be to accept a deprivation in the self which is unnecessary and painful. It often seems to me that work with polarities is the tool *par excellence* for integration.

8
POLARITIES II

I have just given you a paper that I wrote on polarities some while back; in it you will find many of my initial notions about opposites and some of the theoretical frame-work that I found (and still find) essential to the area. Particularly important among these are the concepts of differentiation and integration as espoused by both Jung and Perls, the notion of "archetypes" that often encompass polarities, and the idea of introjects which frequently underlie the polarized parts of the self.

Some of the ideas expressed in the previous paper are useful in conjunction with a lecture on the theory of change and the presentation of the Gestalt attitude toward resistance. In the Gestalt approach, the more one experiences where one is, the more available one is to the process of change; the more aware one is of the *value* as well as the *interfering quality* of resistance, the better one knows oneself and the more capable one is of making choices.

Very simply put, polarities are everywhere. There is nothing recondite or mysterious about their existence. Any day of our lives abounds with them. At this very moment I am polarized. I both want to be here talking to you about polarities (because I'm fascinated with the area—and hope you will be too) and I want to be home in bed with the covers up to my chin (because it's Saturday morning and this is definitely not my time of day). In the same vein, I'm sure there are those of you present who are eager to learn what we—hopefully—have to teach you, and at the same time wish you could be spending the day with your spouse, lover, children, friend. You have, perhaps, some sense of guilt, or

109

a fantasy that you are deserting them—attending to your own needs rather than theirs. Both valid. Both conflicting.

Still remaining in the moment, I can imagine that there are those of you who are split between the desire to pay attention to what's being said and on the other hand the wish merely to sit and simply let my words float by. There may be those of you who would like to get up and move around the room, yet you remain seated because you do not wish to draw attention to yourself nor flout some of the established rules of what passes for acceptable behavior in a "classroom."

Moving somewhat further afield, I can assume that there are those of you here who sometimes (often? always?) experience anger—but stop yourselves form expressing it either because you *fear* your anger itself, the environmental response to your anger, or a loss of control and ultimate dissolution. In the same ballpark there may be those of you who would like to be in therapy, intrigued by the possibilities that it might open for you, but who hold yourself back from entering into it because of the fear of what you might discover, the expectation and anxiety about the changes it might bring. To some of us change is tantamount to death—at least death of the self we have known, loved, hated.

Not all this is nonsense. The therapist too has her polarities, some of them conscious—and as such, paid attention to, regarded with suspicion on occasion, but generally benign. Sometimes, however, these polarities may be unaware, unattended to, and as such may interfere with the client's smooth progression in therapy. For example, if a therapist has a tendency to urge his client to be more assertive at the expense of the milder, more compromising side of his personality, then the client cannot freely explore both sides of himself. And the therapist won't encourage this exploration because he has never come to terms with or recognized *his own* gentleness. This is unfortunate.

What I am trying to do is remove the sense of the arcane from the concept of polarities, make more evident their omnipresence in our world, and hopefully get you in touch with some of your own—both immediate and chronic. Take a minute whenever you can to explore what you conceive of as your personal polarities.

What we usually discover when we are listening or examining polar traits is that one pole is elicited by wishes or wants, whereas the opposite side is contributed to by "shoulds" or "oughts." If we were to think of these poles in psychoanalytical terms, we could compare the two sides of the id and the superego. Fortunately or unfortunately, nothing is quite that clear cut. We do not all have identical opposites (just as we do not all have the same ids and superegos). The opposite of "nice" to one of you might be "not nice", to another, "evil", to another "exciting", to another "ugly", to another "unpleasant", to a sixth "aggressive", and so on, ad infinitum. It's one of the reasons a thesaurus is so useful. But this makes it very important when dealing with polarities never to anticipate or assume that we, as therapists, know what the client acknowledges to himself as his own pole. At the sane time this polarizing provides us with a fantastic tool for widening the scope of the individual's perception. *Providing, of course, that we do not foist our own interpretation on him.*

I was working a few weeks ago with a woman whose mother had cancer. The mother had been in remission for several years but recently was found to be once again in an active stage. Although she was fighting the disease as best she could, availing herself of chemotherapy, and apparently looking forward to another remission, my client could do nothing but anticipate death. She would wish for death rather than the pain her mother was experiencing, and refuse to allow herself to hope—for fear that if she did, she would be devastated when her mother ultimately died. Well, clearly—or not so clearly? —we had a polarity present. Several polarities. The desire to hope, the fear of hoping; the desire for her mother's death (to end her own anxious state), and the fear of that terminal state and permanent loss. All of these conflicts made her unhelpful to her mother, her husband and certainly herself.

Where to go? One of the facts that was vividly present was the pain which she daily inflicted on herself with the expectation that her mother would die presently. True, she would die eventually; so do we all. But to deal with that death as though it might occur each day prevented her from admiring and reinforcing her mother's coping skills or enjoying her immediate presence. We were able, cognitively, to deal with this dilemma; it was certainly evident that unless she shifted her focus no one would benefit. However, though she made some progress in accepting this caveat and even implementing it to a degree, a small voice remained, repeating over and over again: "It is bad to hope."

It was imperative to explain the small voice. When we attended to it and tried to trace its origins, we arrived at the teachings of the Catholic Church which enjoined her to believe that this earth was but a vale of tears, that we must consistently be punished, that no hope was possible while we dwelt here.

I encouraged my client to envision the embodiment of the voice, and to set it bodily in a chair where she could address it. She had trouble doing so because it seemed so amorphous. Eventually she was able to perceive it as a globular monster with a huge head and a negligible body. Engaging in a dialogue with the monster, she (as the monster) reiterated its litany that hope was futile; suffering was all; she was a fool to consider any thing else possible!

Responding as herself—one part of herself—she tried to persuade him (it was a him) that all her experience had showed her otherwise, that hope was healing, that optimism was warranted, that being glad and enjoying the world allowed others to do so as well. But this was to no avail; the monster continued his litany. Suddenly, leaning forward to persuade him more forcefully, she realized her monster had no ears! How could he hear her? What was the point of arguing with something that merely regurgitated cant like a broken record? None. With this realization she was able to recognize that that part of herself—that primitive, early ensconced part—was outmoded, unhelpful and unnecessary to maintain. She experienced a tingling in her fingertips and shook her hands as though to rid herself of something irritating. The monster which she had originally experienced in her stomach had moved to her extremities where, with great glee, she shook him away.

What she had discovered was that her dominant pole—her punitive pole—was an introject, a value she had "swallowed whole" when too young and powerless to know better. As a grown woman with power, integrity and compassion, she could look at it, disagree with it, and decide—for this moment at least—that she could put it aside. Which she did. Her world was suddenly sunny again. Her interactions with her mother were occasions of warmth and acknowledgement. Her husband welcomed her back. And the next week she terminated therapy for the time being. All of us were pleased.

Needless to say, working with polarities does not always provide such dramatic results; many introjects are considerably more ingrained and show up in many areas where they must be dealt with again and again. But looking at them, owning them, acknowledging that they influence both our feelings and our behaviors, allows us to know ourselves a little better and consequently permits us, sometimes, to change.

Several years ago I worked with a young man who, according to the DSM-III categories, was designated obsessive compulsive—a particularly difficult disorder to treat. We managed, over a fairly long period of time, to enable him to deal more effectively with his world. A few weeks ago, after an interim of about three years, he returned to therapy—but not so much obsessive as scared and depressed. Although he possessed a Ph.D. in History and a thorough grasp of his specialty, he was profoundly upset and frightened when one of his students threateningly questioned a test he had given, claiming that it had been designed specifically to flunk him. The accusation was patently untrue, but James was unnerved and found himself not only frightened to lecture but dubious about any of his professional skills. He had come unglued. Almost tearfully, and with some anger, he admitted that he was acting like a child. I asked him, "How old?" "Seven", he replied instantly. So within the man, there was still the child—which is sometimes a delight, but not when it prevents one from functioning. An existing polarity? Perhaps.

What had happened when he was seven? His father, always a difficult man, had started drinking inordinately. He would return from his bouts with the bottle to shout at James' mother, James' sister, and James. He would point out the inadequacies of all those around him—particularly James. He would criticize, demean and lash out. James would cower, hide in his room, tremble, cry—all of these, but he could not protest. Somehow, that bitter, pitiful boy had been revived in the adult James by the incident in his classroom. And there was this boy before me, side by side with the competent man, somehow dwarfing him into insignificance.

I persuaded him to become the little boy and to address the man—to really give voice to his feelings. "I'm scared," he said. "I'm so little, so frail, so unable to stand up for myself. How can I exist in this world?" "Nonsense," replied the man, "That was very long ago. You're very competent now, your body is shaped by different exercise, your mind is sharp. Stop whimpering!" I pointed out that he wasn't attendant to the scared part of him, was not giving the youngster what he needed: acknowledgement, acceptance. He looked startled, but tried again. "I can understand why you're scared; you are little; you can't understand what's happening around you; you can't be expected to stand up to that man. That doesn't make you a coward!" "I know but I feel like one; I just want to ran and hide... there's no one to turn to." "There's me" said the man, "I can keep you safe inside me; I have to remember you're only seven and I am 42."

We still have a long way to go, but I sent him away last week with the task of listing on paper all the things he likes about himself—no mean task. He could only come up with three that day, but we have a beginning—a place to move from.

Try to envision for a moment the self as a globe with a North Pole, a South Pole, an equator and all the points betwixt or between the latitudes and longitudes. If on that globe you place a particular trait, value or way of viewing the world, you can follow that point, three dimensionally, to the other, opposite side of the globe and find its polar trait. So that if at one point you find judgmentalism,

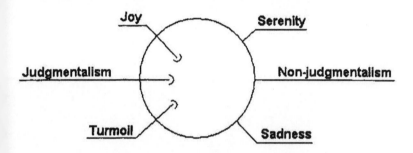

on the other side of the globe you discover non-judgmentalism. If you imagines the line connecting the two, what you finds is a continuum with all the steps between deviating somewhat from one to the other. At any point on our imaginary globe we can place a recognized or disowned trait, only to discover its polar opposite on the other side. It's something like digging a hole to China—or the Chinese digging a hole to us. Yin and Yang.

If we attempt to recognize and explore our many polarities we can discover that there are times when it's useful to operate from one of the poles, times when it behooves us to act from the other, and times when it's profitable to compromise or take a position somewhere other than at the extremes of the continuum (for example, in the polarity of "bullying" versus "cowardice," it may be helpful to explore the region of "taking a firm stand.")

Unless we are able to realize that one quality *presumes* an equal but different quality, we are doomed to narrowness, rigidity, and lack of change and growth. We remain like this sheet of paper—two dimensional. I urge you to explore. If you have never known sadness, it's difficult to recognize joy; if you have never known turmoil, it's hard to recognize serenity. We are defined by our opposites. Without darkness, there can be no light.

9
RESISTANCES

The Gestalt theory of resistance bears some resemblance to Freud's notion of defense mechanisms, but bears also some striking difference. In both instances, resistances—or mechanisms of defense—pertain to ways in which the individual distorts reality in order to preserve some sense of identity, and to evade or avert punishment. But Gestalt and psychoanalytic resistances differ dramatically in the way they are perceived by the therapist and, in turn, by the client.

In psychoanalysis, the therapist's primary task is to break down or break through the resistances of the client. They are regarded as manifestations of the unconscious—in service of the id or super-ego—with the sole purpose of distorting reality in order to preserve the "delusional" system of the individual. Resistances are seen as protective devises, but ones which ultimately must be removed so that "health" can ensue and the ego reign.

The Gestalt therapist, though he too perceives resistances as protective devices, does not consider it necessary to break down or break through them. Rather, she views resistance as a powerful tool in the understanding and eventual development of the total personality—much as Jung views the tension created by opposites as having a formative effect on experience. The Gestalt therapist regards the resistances as a potent source of energy, and chooses to work *with* them rather than *against* them in order to facilitate the expression of a multi-faceted, smoothly functioning human being. In other words, she views resistances as creative forces.

In order to work with resistances it is important to consider what they are and how they may have developed. An individual is not born with a particular resistance. Rather, he learns to resist. At an early age, he learns how to view the world—experimentally—and how to react to that world (from a position of powerlessness) in a way that enables him to survive.

In the process he develops certain unawarenesses of what he does, so that once he has access to power, he may not be able to exercise it. This could occur because he has lost certain awarenesses of the world in which he currently finds himself, or perhaps more importantly: he has lost the awareness of certain parts of himself which may have been dormant for years.

In talking of this lack of awareness—this resistance to contact with both the world and the self—it's important to remember the Reichian concept of "armor". Perls was greatly influenced by Wilhelm Reich and his theory that the resistances took place in the musculature—that all sorts of unawarenesses were maintained by chronic muscular contractions (or "armor") which eventually became unaware. As a result of this armoring, huge amounts of energy could be bound up, unable to flow freely or be accessible to the individual for effective and productive use.

Now the solution, in Gestalt terms, is not simply to break down the armor—though there are other therapies (Alex Lowen) that attempt to do just that—but to get in touch with the resistances and utilize them, in conjunction with the awarenesses, to discover exactly where an individual finds himself at a particular point in time. In doing so, both the client and the therapist gain access to energy that has previously been unavailable or devoted to holding down certain parts of the personality.

A prime example of this holding down process can be viewed in the work with polarities. But to put it quite simply, an individual may be very aware of only one particular side of himself—for example, the side that wishes to fade into the woodwork, to remain unnoticed, to escape the consequences of being seen. What he may not be aware of is his polar opposite—what Jung would term "shadow"—the side of him which would enjoy being exhibitionistic, dramatic, highly visible and loudly applauded. By noticing the actions that accompany his *aware* side (sitting against the wall, hiding his hands, softness or inaudibility in his voice when asked a question, and/or the failure of his eyes to directly focus) we can ask him to experiment with new awarenesses. What would it be like for him to attempt to move away from the wall? To allow his hands to gesture, his voice to grow in volume and his gaze to meet that of another's? If we pursue this we immediately come up against his resistance. After all, it's quite possible that mommy constantly reiterated, "A child should be seen and not heard." But if we confront the resistance, recognize it, allow it a voice of its own, we may arrange for a dialogue to take place between the two sides of the personality which are largely unacquainted with one another. And by exaggerating both sides, the individual may discover the energy in the unexplored part which has been kept under wraps for too long. He may use this energy not necessarily to be exhibitionistic—although he may decide to do that—but to speak up when spoken to, or even to initiate statements that put forth views he never knew he had. In Hegelian terminology he may move from thesis to antithesis to synthesis.

I think it might be wise at this point—before I get carried away entirely with the working of a resistance—to point out as simply as possible those resistances we most often encounter. Moving from the simple to the complex (or, to put it another way, from the most primitive to the most sophisticated), we have: desensitization, introjection, confluence, deflection, projection and retroflection

Each of these resistances—when it is unaware and hence pathological—is ultimately an interruption to contact. To orient us, and to highlight the ways in which you may recognize resistances as interruptions, I will give a very simple definition of each .

119

Desensitization is exactly what it sounds like: it is a numbing-out of sensation, a scotomizing of feeling which at the very beginning of the cycle is a hopeful way of never proceeding beyond the point of initial sensation. With catatonic schizophrenics, for example, desensitization is most evident. (The fact that the catatonic person actually has a great deal of awareness need not at this moment concern us). We can note this particular interruption by observing a lack of motion in the body or some kind of rigidity: the poker face of a client, the holding of the breath, the monotonal quality of the voice, avoidance of specific content (such as sexuality), lack of expressed feeling, not remembering, wanting to work but having little energy.

I recall a client I worked with a while back who manifested almost all of these features. Interestingly he was also very fat; in a sense he had accumulated more and more body armor to maintain his desensitization. When he talked about the depression engendered by living with his wife—ostensibly the figure he was trying to develop—there were no actual signs of the depression nor any energy expressed in his desire to leave her. Over time we focused on many of the interruptions to the feeling of his depression and I particularly remember the break through that came when we attended to the rigidity of his facial muscles. As I gently traced the contours of his face he broke into tears—the first he'd shed in years—and sobbingly spoke of his wife's coldness, her lack of responsiveness and his strong desire for warmth and recognition.

Introjection, in Gestalt terms, means to swallow whole. In the process, the feeling of nausea is subdued and the value, idea, mode of behavior—or whatever is given by the person in power—is allowed to remain undigested in the host's system, where it ultimately does away with all but stereotypic behavior. Instead of being spit out, the introject slowly poisons the system. This resistance shows itself as interruptive—not so much in posture or breathing particularly but in the quality of the person's language—his or her tendency to use cliches, fixed ideas, absolutes, shoulds and oughts. There is also avoidance of expected feelings such as anger and, presumably, confusion—the inability to distinguish what he or she really wants as opposed to what has been introjected.

I'd been working for some time with a very pushy, bright woman who had for several years sacrificed much that she wanted to do for herself in favor of what she thought was required from a mother toward her children. Every time we started to speak of a new career choice for her—once again the uppermost figure—we would get derailed by such statements as, "But a mother's place is in the home," "It's essential that I be there for Johnny when he gets home from school," "There are things that I can do for Jane that no baby sitter can do." All possibly true—but said as if taped, canned, non-spontaneous.

It became imperative to separate out what she really believed from that which she had swallowed whole before we could move with her uppermost figure. In the process, of course, the figure changed and we spent many sessions exploring which part of her represented "mama" and which part represented her own position at the present time. We used dialogue, work with polarities, conversations about the rearing of children before we got to the point where she could accept that unless she took care of herself, she could not be truly available in spontaneous ways for her children. At the point at which that happened we were able to move back to the figure of career choice and concentrate on it without the same kind of interruptions.

Confluence means literally to "flow along with." In effect one goes with the current, with the ideas, wants, behaviors of the other so that conflict is avoided and boundaries are not established. One does not have a chance to assert who one is. When I attempt to distinguish confluence from introjection, I perceive it as operating at a slightly more aware level.

As an interruption, confluence can often be recognized through body posture. You might note that a confluent client imitates the way in which you, yourself, are sitting. It can be seen in a smiling face (particularly when the smile does not fit the content), in a rate of speech similar the therapist's, and in the consistent agreement with what the therapist says (even though this may contradict what the client had reported previously). Confluence is also implicated when the client only expresses feelings that are expected to be approved of—so that anger, for example, rarely gets exposed. When confluence is predominant, withdrawal difficulties are experienced and inconsistencies between systems abound.

No matter what a confluent client presents, a figure can rarely be developed as long as the client remains in a state of confluence. In addition, this kind of client can be deadly dull. Since there's no conflict, there's no tension and consequently no excitement. One man I worked with agreed with everything I said so that I finally resorted to saying nothing at all—a very difficult thing for me to do. Of course when I did this, he inevitably became silent too. And he also became angry. I could note this in his rigid posture, his clenched hands and the tension in his face. His anger gave me something to focus on, which prompted at least two things: 1) his resistance to getting angry because he believed it would elicit anger in turn, and 2) his excessive need for everyone to like him. What we had to confront was the fallacy of his premises and the fact that constant agreement is boring, boring, boring! There was also the question of what his dullness did for him—and with that we had a figure.

Deflection means specifically "to turn aside," to change the subject, to vary the mood, to laugh or smile inappropriately— in effect, to prevent a remark or an action from hitting its target. Deflection as an interruption to an emerging figure can be seen in an many ways: fidgeting, excessive tension while someone else is speaking, coughing or making other sounds which appear inappropriate, too many words with too few silences, frequent interruptions of the self so that the topic keeps changing and incoherent data keeps being introduced, evasive humor, "tunnel vision", figure-ground problems—you name it.

All or any of these interruptions may occur in one-on-one therapy, but they are particularly obtrusive when one is working with a couple. I started working with a new couple a few weeks ago. They've been married about 15 years with a minimum of stress. But the man's sister had just moved into town and decided to run their lives (as she had little of her own to manage). This was ostensibly no problem for the man, who had grown up with her and learned to ignore everything with which he disagreed. Fighting was not in his vocabulary. But it was most disruptive to the woman who was constantly confrontative. When she wasn't confronting the sister she was arguing with the man about the sister until the marriage was, indeed, in jeopardy. Both their styles were evident in their initial interview with me, but most apparent was the wife's marked tendency to deflect.

Whenever the husband would attempt to make a point about their relationship, she would turn to me—avoiding his eyes—and launch into a tirade about the sister-in-law. I really didn't want to hear about the sister-in-law; I wanted to focus on the system that existed between the two of them. But her diatribes certainly gave me a clue as to what was happening. Each time she interrupted his emerging feeling or thought and went off on her own, he became quiet, looked down at his hands and sometimes laid his head in them. She went blithely on. When I pointed out their behavior he indicated that it occurred constantly and that essentially he could not think of any way to interrupt her interruptions. True, he was not assertive. But there are non-aggressive ways of asserting oneself—yet he couldn't think of any. So I pointed out their respective sitting positions, particularly the short distance from his right hand to her left thigh—and the possibility of his bringing that hand to rest on that thigh. Could he try that? He could. He did. When asked what her response to his gesture was, she responded immediately that she was calmed, that her attention was riveted on him and that she felt attended to—a very nice beginning.

Projection is the inability *to accept as one's own* an impulse, feeling or desire that originates in the self. Consequently, the impulse, feeling or desire is attributed to someone or something in the environment, and is then experienced as being directed back toward the self.

There are ways in which we can recognize the projection process as it interrupts concentration on—or development of—the uppermost figure. Posturally, our projector is on the look out, possibly sitting on the edge of his chair, eyes fixed on the other, finger sometimes pointing. His voice may sound accusatory or defensive depending on the content of what he is saying. At the same time his language may be impersonal, full of intellectualization, sprinkled with "it appears that," "we feel that," "they say that...". There is rarely any high degree of ownership; rather there are assumptions and projections. Accordingly the person rarely learns from his mistakes since the blame for any miscalculation or catastrophe is consistently placed on someone else. Ironically, so is the praise for any of her successes. As a result she is often impatient and irritable.

Not too long ago I was working with a client who was a projector par excellence. In addition, he was addicted to drugs—a ghastly combination. He blamed his professors for his difficulties in school, his landlord for his difficulty with the other tenants, his wife for making it impossible for him to give up drugs. Whenever we would start to develop a figure moving toward his own instrumentality in his poor relationships, he would move into his projective mode, and there we were back with his professor, his landlord, his wife. Heightening his "it" language was of some value, asking him to never shift his gaze from mine brought some awareness, but it wasn't until we started using his dreams as projected facets of himself that we made any real progress. In the dream-work he began to re-own the disowned parts of the self.

Retroflection means to turn sharply against the self that which rightfully should be directed toward the environment. In the process the retroflector splits himself into two parts, the subject and the object; he both does and is done to. The individual who uses retroflection as his chief mechanism for interruption or resistance can be identified easily by an abundance of bodily movements. She may drum her fingers on the arm of a chair, slowly swing one leg over the other, chew on her fingernails or the inside of her cheeks, bite her lips, hug herself with her own arms, clench her fists or become totally rigid.

A retroflector may smile inappropriately when what he is saying calls for tears or anger; he may hold his breath, blame, pity, get angry with himself rather than the other, avoid arguing, yelling, and expressing a desire for sex; and he may show up at your office with a host of psychosomatic symptoms.

A woman I am working with currently sits rigidly in her chair while she talks about how much she misses her husband who died about a year ago. Her eyes fill with tears as she tells me how good he was to her and how she didn't deserve his kindness. As her voice breaks, her hands clench and I wonder who she'd like to hit or choke. I don't verbalize this, but I do comment on her clenched hands. This is followed by a torrent of angry words describing how he left her with no insurance, how he never stuck up for her to his relatives, how he questioned the purchases she made for herself. When I ask her to visualize him in the other chair and tell him these things, she freezes again and replies, "Oh, I'm just petty, I guess; he really was a good guy." But unless I keep noticing her non-verbal (and verbal) clues and keep heightening them, she is going to continue directing her anger at herself and continue to maintain her depression. The uppermost figure of her valid anger will be blurred so that we will not be able to develop a direction in which she can move.

As I have said, these are the pathological definitions— resistances as *interruptions* to contact. But it's most important to remember that each of the resistances can be viewed in a healthy light as well. To turn off one's sexuality—to *desensitize* oneself— when there is no suitable object might cause discomfort, but might also be the most adaptive and creative response in a particular situation.

The ability to swallow something whole may likewise be a valuable skill. Introjecting a lecture containing information that may need to be spewed forth on an exam (and serves no other learning purpose) may be an expedient way to learn something which is important only for the moment (like Latin verbs).

To go along with someone's wishes or ideas when it does not take away from the self to do so—and when it might alienate someone important if you refuse—can be useful. To flow along with a loved one after orgasm, when one wishes to be part of another—and to hell with boundaries—is a joyous experience.

To "take the heat off" a potentially explosive situation by cleverly changing the subject, or injecting a soupçon of humor, may save a marriage or prevent a war.

To read into another's behavior, feelings of pain or discomfort, because one has felt them oneself, is projective. But the example makes clear that projection is a part of empathy, without which there might be no marvelous friendships or creative art forms.

To comfort oneself by taking a bubble bath, or treating oneself to a glass of wine when there is no one else around to do it for you can be sustaining; to freeze one's anger instead of directing it at the policeman who is giving one a ticket could save you an appearance in court.

In short (although it's beginning to feel long): to use any of the resistances with a modicum, if not a maximum, amount of awareness is a productive thing to do. It is this *awareness* which we try to foster. In Gestalt therapy the resistances which concern us are those which are *unaware*, those which are not being *chosen* in the present as ways of coping even though they *originated* as coping mechanisms. These resistances are ways of being that are now outmoded and interfering rather than useful.

Our job as therapists is to determine whether a resistance is aware or unaware, chosen or stereotypic, and to treat them accordingly. Those which are aware and useful we support; those which are chronic and interruptive of growth we attempt to bring into awareness. We do this gently if possible, persistently if difficult—but always to increase the options of the individual who constantly needs to enlarge his repertoire of behaviors if he is to continue to grow, or in Maslow's terms, to become more nearly self-actualized.

To aid in this process we move in infinitesimal increments, rarely taking huge leaps into the unknown, always anchoring our moves and so-called intuitions onto small clues and phenomenological data. An ancillary mode of procedure can be found in Bandler and Grinder's *Structure of Magic* (1975), which could more simply have been called the "Structure of Language or Grammar". It is always important to know who, what, when, where, and how as one is listening and exploring an individual's revelations or resistances. Indeed, the important rules of simple journalism equally apply.

I remember re-reading Hannah Green's *I Never Promised You a Rose Garden* and being exquisitely aware that the therapist in the book was in actuality the renowned psychiatrist Frieda Fromm-Reichmann. I was also aware that the patient so vividly described presented all of the resistances we have been talking about today, and that the process used to effect a return to reality was always that of making her aware—of her strengths, of her resistances. I was profoundly touched.

In closing I'd like to reaffirm some of Perls' early ideas about resistance. As I remember it, he said that avoidance is a general factor found in every neurotic mechanism and that seldom—actually only in cases of real and tangible danger—is anything gained by this avoidance. A civil war is often raging in the neurotic organism between the motoric system—which is moved to freeze and armor the individual—and the organismic energies struggling for expression and gratification. Needless to say, I'm on the side of the latter.

10
ENERGY AND EXPERIMENT

When I'm asked to talk about experiment, particularly experiment that utilizes both active and receptive energy, I think first of how experiment relates to life itself—to the themes that fill and round out a life time—and the risks we, as individuals, take to move ourselves from a passive thinking about to an active risk-taking stance which enables us to push apart our boundaries.

I'm aware that there are certain types of therapy that in essence never draw upon experiment to foster growth and that—even so—clients sometimes grow. But it seems to me that to neglect experimentation deprives a therapist of a most valuable part of her armamentarium. And it deprives the client of experiencing himself in a new and perhaps frightening way in a low risk situation.

Experiments in a therapeutic situation are not playthings that we normally use at the very beginnings of sessions—although there are certainly exceptions to this. Rather they are tools that emerge out of the activity or passivity of a client over long periods of time and out of our receptivity to their modes of being, their themes if you will, and our own active sharing of our process. I recall vividly a man I worked with who over many sessions smiled solicitously every time he talked about incidents which made him angry. At first I was only receptive to his content and responding on that level, but gradually I became aware of a growing feeling of discomfort at the incongruence between his words and his expression, and further of a sense that he was trying to prevent me

129

from reacting to him as an angry man by wearing the mask of a jolly one.

I finally shared my process with him and wondered aloud—actively—whether he was trying to fool the rest of his world in the same way. At first he denied that he was smiling, then admitted to it as I asked him to feel his face, but again denied that he was trying to hide his anger. So I had him imagine his wife in a chair and direct his angry words to her. He did so—smilingly. We had discovered one of his modes of being in the world, one of his themes. You'll notice that in this particular instance the experiment came before the client's development of a theme—which is at odds with the way we sometimes teach theme and how the energy inherent in that theme leads to experiment (a "thematic experiment").

The latter is clearly true; in the development of a theme one flushes out the need or want and in examining the details that surround that need one also stumbles on the resistance which frequently leads to an impasse, a need for direction and hopefully an experiment. But in the man I discussed just previously, a theme per se was implicit in the incongruity of his behavior, and the experiment evolved without much preamble. It was, indeed, and experiment; I may have had a hypothesis, but I certainly had no conclusion in mind. Rather, I was willing to deal with whatever emerged and so to support his experience even if that involved his anger being directed toward me. Always bear in mind *your own resistance* when doing experiments. If you have the clear or even amorphous feeling that you will not be able to handle that which you actively evoke—pass. Do something else. Grade your investigation down to something you can cope with comfortably. Find out, for example, what your client feels about your observations. This strategy may take you in the direction of interpersonal interaction—which is good!

I'd really like to divide and talk about experiments in two ways: the experiments that evolve from themes and how we deal with them; and the experiments that derive from a pattern of behavior (as did the one I cited above)—a physical movement, perhaps, or merely a word that grabs you in a particular way—in other words, an awareness experiment.

Experiments that evolve from themes follow a particular structure and usually involve a series of steps. First, it's important to know that there is a clarity to the theme—both for yourself and for your client. In other words, be sure you're talking about the same thing, be it responsibility, sexuality, problems with authority or how to live with one's devils—pride, arrogance, greed. Be sure the theme is your client's and not your own.

You can determine that you've picked up on the client's theme from the amount of energy *your client* invests in the interaction—not the amount *you* do, although that too is important. Once you're confident that you're on the right track, it's time to propose your experiment and to get consent for it. Say you're working with a young man who has definite problems with authority; every time he has to have a conference with his advisor (or his boss, or his father) his stomach ties itself in knots—or to put it more precisely, he ties his stomach in knots—and his palms start to sweat. What he ostensibly wants is to deal with authority, to not have problems with it, not to knot up his stomach, not to have palms that sweat. Very well, there are numerous directions in which you can move. But whichever one you choose, be very clear about what you would like your client to do. For example, spell out that you'd like him to play two parts: that of himself and that of his advisor. Spell out that he should visualize himself in one chair and his advisor in another. Spell out that you want him to have a dialogue between the two characters and that he should move from one chair to the other as he speaks the lines emanating from the speaker in that particular chair. At this point you'd do well to bring your active self into the work.

It is important to make sure that—even though *you* think this is a great experiment—your client thinks so as well. If it's clear that he does, if he consents to do it because it energized him as well as you, then essentially you have a contract and may proceed. A contract, not a confluence.

If, on the other hand, he is not energized, or doesn't feel enough support, or feels the risk is too great or too small, the contract can be amended and the experiment graded up or down—or dropped entirely. To grade an experiment up you may either increase the risk or decrease the support. To grade it down you decrease the risk or increase the support.

In this particular instance if the client had felt it too risky to play both parts in the dialogue, I could have lowered that risk by offering to play one of the parts, or I could have given him more support by offering to be his alter ego and back him up with lines that he could use in his dialogue. Another way of lowering that risk is to ask him to play it out in fantasy and see what happens.

As it happened my client was quite willing to try to experiment and got a really exciting dialogue going between himself and his advisor. Interestingly, although he was normally a fairly forthright young man when talking to me, he became excessively meek when "playing" himself. The advisor, on the contrary, was played as a veritable tyrant who certainly did not advise but practiced brow-beating instead. It was also interesting that as the tyrant became more tyrannical, the client became less and less meek until he was matching him insult for insult, demand for demand, and ultimately stating that he, the client, wanted the position of the advisor for himself! Gone were the sweaty palms, gone the knots in the stomach. High and vital was the energy. And a new direction was clear: turn a rather mild though forthright young man into someone aware of his own power and his potential ability to use it.

I'll give another example. A man comes into my office with a stomachache. He's eaten nothing that disagrees with him, he doesn't believe he's sick, he feels unenergized. Actually his energy is directed toward his own pain; he is being receptive to it. And I am receptive to both his content and his process, which mobilizes me to listen to my insides and come up with an experiment. I'm remembering that the diaphragmatic armor which includes the stomach is often expressed in nausea and an attitude of "no-no" to life. But how to approach this without literally undoing the armor? Once more I take initiative; I begin by asking him to imagine himself very small, and to take a trip down into his stomach to discover what he finds there...

This time I had a hypothesis, but I had no specific idea of where we would end up—that had to be discovered through the experiment, which led through pain, to loneliness, to sharing, to the diminution of pain. His pain was something which he had to discover on his own through a fantasy trip. It was exciting, moving, fulfilling for us both. And once again we have a theme.

How many times when you ask a client an important question do you get the response, "I draw a blank"? They draw a blank because their resistance to a need at that moment is greater than the ability to *share* that need, that want. But have you ever asked them to actually draw the blank? To fill it in, as they might in their mind's eye—much as they would a cartoon strip? I'm amazed sometimes as to how that cuts through the resistances—focusing on their word, taking them by surprise. And occasionally taking me by surprise.

I remember vividly a time when a young man I was working with "drew a blank." He was a most attractive young man but withdrawn, cool, always taking the chair in my office furthest from mine. Never asking for anything. On this particular day he was more withdrawn than ever, more silent than ever, and yet the room somehow crackled with energy. I bestirred myself to remark on his silence, his withdrawal and my feeling that something important was going on inside him. I asked him if there was anything he wanted from me—I being the only other person in the room—and he replied, "I draw a blank". So I had him draw it, and then I had him fill it in, slowly, with people and things and ambience. And what he came up with was a snowy mountain with a small cabin near the summit, and in the cabin was a brightly burning fire and a brightly colored rug with a deep soft weave and nothing else but him—and me. I don't know which of us was more surprised. Diagnostic? Indeed. A one dimensional, noncommunicative male had revealed depths of brightness and softness and glowing energy and deep wanting that he had forbidden himself to know. A lifetime theme? Perhaps. But I want to emphasize again that when you undertake an experiment you truly need to be prepared for the unexpected, because an experiment is a means of exploration, the ending of which is unknown. And sometimes the ending involves you—me—us.

I could go on offering you examples—there are so many—but let me add only that experiments come in many forms. Pick ones that feel comfortable for you. Pick from dramatization—psychodrama, acting out, empty chairs; from directed behavior—"Behave in a certain way, different perhaps from your usual one"; from structured fantasy—using the material your client has brought in; from dream-work—a whole special area that is demanding and rewarding; from free fantasy—"Take a trip..."; or from awareness experiments in which you encourage the person to use his senses in a new way to explore his world.

I have tried today to focus on experiment in the light of energy—active and receptive—but I'd like to remind you that there are other focal points to consider regarding experiments. It's extremely important to pay attention to these considerations:

1) How much tension is there in the system—and where? If there's not enough, one can't produce; if there's too much, there's the possibility of immobilization.

2) What is the want or impulse involved—in other words, what organizes the energy?

3) Where—or what—are the resistance points, the points where the work has to be active?

And some pieces of advice:

1) play off the client's own words.

2) the final action of the experiment should be related to the opening impulse—thus completing a unit of work.

3) Work slowly; heighten the resistance—if there is no resistance there is no growing edge.

Remember: you and your client are a system. Just as the embers in the fireplace have to be fanned to flame, and a poker must be used to move a log so that it can catch—since one log alone cannot burn—so your energy and that of your client must compliment and build upon one another in order for experiments to burgeon and worlds enlarge.

11
OBSERVATION AND
AWARENESS

When we speak of observation, we are speaking in essence of awareness—*how* to be aware and *what* to be aware of. When you're in the observer role in a practice triad, your primary awareness is directed toward the therapist: how she functions or doesn't function, how she establishes contact or does not establish contact with her patient. Needless to say, if you do not become aware of the patient as well, you have no data to tell you what in is actually happening in the total situation.

Awarenesses occur through the use of the senses—sight, hearing, smell, touch and taste. In observing the therapist in a practice triad, you are more or less restricted to sight and hearing, though there are moments when the smell of fear may be palpable. This is not too bad a deprivation—there are a great number of things that may be seen or heard. If you are sitting in the right position (and it's important to do so) you can see the expression on the face of the therapist—or the absence of expression. You may also see the expression on the face of the patient in response to that expression, or in avoidance of that expression or in simple ignorance of it because he is looking somewhere else.

In giving feedback to the therapist it's not particularly fruitful to say, "You looked amused at something your client said and she in turn looked angry." Both "amused" and "angry" are interpretative words; more useful would be, "Your eyes crinkled at the corners and one side of your mouth moved upward when

137

Lucy said she was a real loser. Then Lucy tightened her lips and drew her brows together. When you called attention to her expression, she shrugged it away." With that sort of data both therapist and patient may recapture the moment in question and check out what happened to them at that moment. For example, the therapist may not have been aware that he was looking amused (it may be that he has a habitual way of covering over his feelings when some one else is playing themselves down.) If his precise behavior is pointed out to him he may be alerted for it the next time.

In the same way, saying that the therapist looked disinterested in something his client said, and that the client then became lethargic doesn't have the same impact as saying, "Your face remained impassive while Lucy was talking and your eyes wandered to a spot on the wall."

Faces may wear any number of varied expressions: joy, sadness, elation, hostility, tenderness, interest, boredom—but each one of these words is an interpretation of the muscular movement that comprises it. We're interested in the data of the muscular movement because it's non-evaluative and specific.

This same approach may be used when dealing with body expression or movement. Again, instead of relating that the therapist seemed uninvolved in his client's dilemma, you might point out that all the time Janie was hammering out her story by pounding on the arm of her chair and leaning toward the therapist, he in turn leaned back in his chair with his hands dangling at his sides and his eyes half closed. Perhaps this was followed by Janie huddling up in a ball and lowering her head to her chest. Or it might be that a different type of client pounds on the therapist's knee instead of her own. What we're trying for is a specificity of language rather than vague generalizations. In this way, we can illuminate the process of what is going on between therapist and patient, and discover whether or not contact is being made—and how. We can see facial expressions, body expressions and movements; we can see quickness of gestures, slowness of gestures, moving toward and away or no movement at all. We can see direction of gaze, steadiness of gaze, wandering of eyes or staring, and to all these things in the visual dimension we can observe a response.

In the dimension of hearing there are also a number of things which one may train oneself to be aware of. There is the loudness or softness of a tone of voice, there is a harshness or breathiness, there is a rise and fall of cadence, a melody or a monotony of inflection. There is a rapidity or slowness with which one moves from phrase to phrase, there is a tightness in the throat as if one's voice is being strangled—there is a silence. All these things one may hear if one's ear is good—all these things in *addition* to the words that are used.

And what about the words? They may be pungent words which please with their aptness or mundane words tired with repetition. They may be words that verge on metaphor or poetry, or factual words which tell it like it is. They may be words that surprise with their unexpectedness or words that summarize with clarity; words that affirm or words that deny, or for that matter words which merely show that one hasn't listened. All of these may be observed—and, in turn, the response evoked by them. Above all, we may attend to the congruence (or lack of it) between words and tone, expression and movement.

Needless to say, as the observer is noticing the therapist's behavior, the therapist is noticing her client's. However, instead of writing her observations down in a notebook (as the observer does), the therapist may share her awareness with her client (which is one way of making contact) or she may react to it (which is another) or she may decide to store it away for future reference. She may, of course, do nothing at all—not always the best way of making contact.

I'd like to reintroduce at this point the awareness, excitement, action cycle. If you recall, this cycle may be interrupted at any point. If it is interrupted before awareness, the subject (be he therapist or observer) is somehow blocking off the functioning of his senses toward the outside world—he may be so focused on himself that he doesn't know what's happening out there. If the cycle is interrupted before excitement, the subject experiences immobilization rather than tumescence and warmth. When interrupted before action, the need which is experienced is not expressed (not communicated) and so excitement is turned into anxiety and constriction.

It is the excitement part of this cycle which is one of the therapist's choice vehicles of communication and, consequently, contact. In watching student therapists therapize, one of the things I'm keenly aware of is the ways in which many of them dampen their excitement. They hold themselves rigid in their chairs, they dull the sparkle in their eyes, they stop their voices from quavering or breaking or their laughter from peeling out. All this rather than the action that comes with excitement: banging one's heels on the floor or slapping one's hand down on a desk or just shouting "hurrah" when the spirit moves one. By imposing an iron-clad control over their own behavior—control which they somehow label as "therapeutic"—they model the same kind of control for their client. This may be quite desirable in the case of a manic person, but more usually it is stifling. Therapy is to be enjoyed. I don't mean by that that it's never to be painful, but I do mean that it's to be experienced—by therapist and client—in a real interchange of feeling. Therapy is not a disguise of feelings in the service of rationality or ill-advised control. The latter is usually interpreted by the client as phony.

I would like you all to be on the *qui vive* for the control that masks excitement or insecurity or trepidation—not so as to get carried away by that same excitement, insecurity or trepidation but so that you know it's there to be tapped as a contact vehicle. The therapist can spot it in himself by his quick heart beat, his holding of his breath, his clammy hands, the prickling on his skin or his scalp; the observer may spot it in the ebb or the flow of blood to the face, the tapping of a finger on the arm of a chair, a quick drawn breath; or he may deduce it from his own experience of similar emotions, often a most accurate projective device.

I want to state very clearly that the sharing of insecurity and trepidation is not always a vehicle of contact. It can sometimes blow a precarious situation absolutely sky high. For example, if a client with a very shaky grip on his own reality is experiencing chaotic movement in his head and is freaking out with the experience, sharing with him your own fear that he's going to flip his lid is less than useful. More important is to get him in touch with his ability to slow down his process by instructing him as to how to breathe and how to focus on outer objects instead of inner movement. But in order to do that—to get him in touch with his own controls—you have to use your own contact functions: a voice that directs with firmness and power, a hand that grips a shaking knee with assurance and strength, and eyes that look assuredly. Just as awarenesses are garnered through the senses, so contact can be made by appealing to them.

What I'm trying to say is that there will be many kinds of data available to you as you work in a triad. If you are the therapist, there will be the sight, sound, smell, touch and kinesthetic sense of your client, plus your own autonomic, emotional and cognitive responses. If you are the observer you will be met by the sight, sound and kinesthetic sense of both the therapist and client, in addition to your own gut-level reactions (for which you'll have no outlet but your pen and notebook, and perhaps some catharsis later). Certainly a plethora of goodies. The object of all this is to learn, to give feedback that is illuminating and cogent, to practice being aware and getting in touch, and to develop a style through the liberty of making mistakes. To stretch your boundaries—if you will.

12
THEME

In the past several chapters, we have moved from an introduction to Gestalt therapy through the cycle of experience and some of its resistances, to sensation and awareness—both inner and outer—and have approached a point where it appears reasonable and useful to talk about theme as an organizer of awareness.

When I think about theme as a concept, I am flooded with messages from my own appreceptive mass—from the vast, background pool of experience that comprises my life space. I think of themes that have moved me in literature, particularly those I encountered in myths and fairy tales. Heroic themes in which there was always a need and a striving for something magnificent which somehow was thwarted by outside forces or a "tragic flaw" within the hero himself (Hamlet attempting to avenge the death of his father but always stopped by his own musings, his own indecision—Semele's need to view her lover, Zeus, in all his glory but dying because her humanity could not tolerate his Godliness).

I think of themes in music, some of which make an appearance, move into variations and then on to another theme, as happens so often in the classical symphonies, such as those of Brahms. Or on the other hand the pervasive theme in Ravel's Bolero that starts softly, swells to a crescendo, but essentially never varies or gives way to another major theme.

I think of the dictionary definition of theme which derives from the Greek word *thema* meaning "what is laid down," and more appropriately for our purposes, a recurring, unifying subject or idea; a motif—a way in which we recognize a song, a story, a work of art. Pissarro's themes, for example, dealt with the land, the peasants, the natural beauty of the country near and around Paris; Renoir's frequently dealt with the symmetry and softness of the female form; Miro's with sheer color and abstract form *per se*.

In Gestalt therapy we view theme as a schema or screen through which we perceive our lives. They are the stories we tell ourselves in the dark of the night and the sometimes painful dawn to make some sense out of our experience. These stories we tell ourselves, these myths, beliefs, fairy tales that we live by are the best possible ones we can evolve, *but* they can be full of contradictions or represent a reality that has faded long ago—a mother that was cold and forbidding who is now attempting warm overtures, a father who was never home but who is currently trying to visit, to get to know you. A client's theme, often implicitly stated or expressed, leads to the polarities, the blocking, the contradictions, the dilemmas he is dealing with.

Stop for a moment and consider what the word "theme" means to you. Bear in mind that the meanings you come up with can be personal, social, political, or cultural; there is no sense of limits when we think in thematic terms. Anything goes; there is no good or bad theme. There are merely themes that speak of who or where you are or have been at various points in your life...

Looking at theme as organization of awareness we may state that theme is *the distilled essence of the client's concern*. It integrates the work of the session. In a sense it provides a unifying thread, a story line, a script if you will.

The theme points the way that the session may take. As it gathers momentum, there is a growing excitement in both therapist and client; nothing is static. *Contact* is required between client and therapist, and if we're lucky an "ah-ha" phenomenon may occur. One might say that this moment—this ah-ha experience—is the best moment of therapy; that it is, in effect, a breakthrough.

What I am going to define for you now is "theme" as we have come to look at it in Gestalt terms. It is not a definition that you will find in the work of Perls because it was developed over time here at the Institute. It provides us with a way of looking at therapy so that we may focus on a unit of work rather than tracking or simply moving with the flow, which ultimately can lead to confluence.

Theme is uppermost figure—a figure composed of a need/want—*plus* direction. It is not a vase or a window or even another person in the room, although all of these may possess the attributes of figure as we have learned them. Without the essential qualities of need/resistance coupled with direction, they remain figure—not theme. I emphasize this because again and again—in the halls—I hear students questioning, "But what is the difference?" Theme, if theme it is, raises energy—Perls' notion of excitement. It is where the energy is located—or where that same energy is blocked. A theme illustrates in its fullness *where* or *how* we stop ourselves. Included in this *where* and this *how* are the qualities that formulate and give birth to the direction to be taken. Again, without this *direction* we do not have theme; we may at best have uppermost figure.

Let me try to illustrate this in therapeutic terms. Say that a client arrives at a therapy session in the depths of despondency. His despair, anguish and depression are figural. They are not new; he has arrived in the same state time and time again. All by itself this depression is not yet a theme. If we look at it more closely, give the client time and room to elaborate, we may discover those factors—those figures—that make up the despair.

On the one hand our client may desperately need/want a new loved one to be a permanent, important, necessary part of his life. His eyes may light up when he talks of her, his energy may soar. But very quickly he is besieged by guilt—the pressure (bred in the bone) to return to the family he has left because he found little satisfaction in the marriage. What we have, of course, is a need and a strong resistance to that need—the conflict between the two giving us uppermost figure.

What we do *not* have yet is a direction—and there are many directions we could take. We could explore the resistance—move into the past to discover when or how the guilt was generated. Perhaps it comes from a mother or father who felt keeping the family together at any price—never mind warmth, never mind love, never mind communication—was the only way to be in the world.

We could move into experiment (which ultimately is where theme leads), encourage our client to confront his mother and tell her, probably with tears, how her messages to him left him with no sense of self but only a sense of duty; how it left him with no expectation of warmth and support but merely of cool tolerance.

We could explore the need, and design ways in which it could be met without the loss of everything else—in other words, the middle ground where he could *fantasize* how his new love might give to his children things that he and his wife haven't been able to provide enough of: spontaneity, directness, an open way of being in the world.

Or we could work the polarities—have the need speak to the resistance—and the resistance speak back, so that the introjects, projections, and retroflections could surface.

Any one of these directions coupled with the identified uppermost figure would provide us with a theme that would give impetus and direction to the therapy session. But it must be a direction that has energy for both the client and the therapist. If you, as therapist, foist a direction on a client, he will be doing your work—if he consents to do it at all—and the energy will plummet.

It's important to bear in mind that theme is a phenomenon of the therapy *interaction*. Therefore theme development is a complex process which includes:

1. The therapist's formulation of energized figure
2. An assessment of client's energy regarding that figure
3. A statement by the therapist to the client of the current figure and direction
4. The client's response
5. If necessary, a modification of the theme so that both therapist and client are engaged by it

Stating the theme marks the therapist's transition from attending and tracking the client's process to the taking of a more active stance. In doing this, the therapist begins to generate the possibility of a new experience for the client (for example, by using the theme to set up an experiment).

Theme development is a particular way of functioning which bounds the experience of the therapy. It serves several functions:

1. It organizes what is happening within a manageable unit
2. It connects client and therapist with an agreed-upon focus
3. It raises energy so that the figure becomes more lively
4. It begins to develop a direction for action
5. It is the ground work for experiment

It follows that there are a number of things that theme is not: theme is *not* interpretation; nor is it is a definition of goals or a summary of content. Rather, theme is a unifier of experience—a method of taking ideas, values and stories about the self that may have existed in logic-tight compartments, and opening the doors between the compartments so that boundaries become permeable and one part of the self may meet another.

Themes may vary in size from mini- to grand to meta- (all encompassing lifetime themes). They may reoccur over time, being played over and over again in a myriad of different ways at various times and at different stages of one's life. They are expansive; they may begin at a personal level and move from there to a couple, a family system, a community, a culture.

There is a vast difference between theme as used in Gestalt and theme as used in other therapies. In Psychoanalysis there are pre-conceived themes with pre-ordained solutions. Behavioral therapy sets up specific goals and thereafter works in a straight line. Rogerian therapy leaves out the relationship with the therapist and deals only with the client's expressed content.

In Gestalt Therapy we can tell if a theme is pertinent by the energy mobilized, because *if it is pertinent* it will intrinsically mobilize energy. You can see or hear the energy by attending to the musculature, the voice, the overall look of aliveness—or implosion. If the theme is not clear, energy becomes fragmented and diffused, and if the theme is too scary, energy turns into resistance. In addition, it is harder to get to an absence of energy than to energy itself. One needs to pay attention to one's own sense of absence. To do so you must take into account your gut feelings—your own needs and wants.

The use of theme is the specific art of the Gestalt therapist. It is a creative projection—the ability to know and own something in yourself and to identify that something in another. It is the ability to be aware of not knowing it in the self and still be able to "lovingly investigate it in another with respect and with wonderment."

Given all this, we now find ourselves with a beginning a middle and an end. We have a road map for the therapy process. We can know at all times where we are and where it is necessary to go.

13
WITHDRAWAL AND CLOSURE

Everything has its season; there is a time for beginnings and a time for endings, a time to start and a time to stop. Sometimes slowly, with lingering and reluctance—sometimes abruptly and sharply with decisiveness.

I am very aware, when I look at training groups, that I was there at their inception. I remember vividly the slow uncongealing of what was an amorphous group into vivid singular images of a particular fact that stood out for me, a characteristic stance that drew my attention, the various sounds of voices that moved into my space, the scent of someone's perfume that differentiated her from the rest of the group.

In a sense, groups like these come full circle. I end with them as I began. But the members are no longer merely ground—unfamiliar, available to be discovered. Rather, as I allow my gaze to wander from one to another participant, each in turn becomes figural—not in a new way necessarily, but replete with the learnings we have formed together. Replete with the myriad facets of members known somewhat by the myriad facets of me.

So given this particular point in time, given the attention we devote to the cycle of experience, I'd like to discuss withdrawal and closure—not my favorite subject in the world. Nonetheless, in doing this, it is important to remember that although withdrawal as a resistance may occur at any point in the cycle (one may withdraw from sensation, from awareness, from excitement, from action, from contact and, indeed, from closure), one may only have closure if one has had *contact*, either with another person or object or with oneself. In other words one must have completed the cycle.

When you are finishing with a group, look around the room for a moment—slowly. Pay attention to those individuals in the room with whom you have become more than strangers, those individuals whom you have allowed to share in your world and who have permitted you a share in theirs. Is your impulse to quickly turn away in order to prevent the wrenching pangs of parting? Or do you choose to linger in your looking, attempting to savor one additional time the nourishment that is there? Or do you hang on for dear life to that which is in reality completed and needs to be put away for at least a while?

As you look again at those individuals with whom you believe you have shared contact experiences, consider for a moment whether your experience indeed conformed to the primary definitions of contact. In other words, whether it provided for the awareness of and behavior toward the assimilable novelty and the movement away and rejection of the unassimilable novelty. For in the process of assimilation the organism is changed—all contact is a creative adjustment of the organism and the environment. Growth is the function of the contact boundary in the organism-environment field. So, as you look around, consider whether you have grown with or because of the person you are looking at or whether instead your relationship was one of confluence, of maintaining the status quo.

I do not mean to imply by what I have said so far that contact *per se* (and withdrawal and closure as its aftermath) is always, or even often, a major experience. The cycle of experience is in actuality only one ring of an ever extending process. It may be seen not simply as a circle but, more accurately, as a spiral—with each ring representing various needs, major or minor, in the need-fulfillment pattern. One may contact and withdraw from any number of small needs in the process of achieving larger ones. An example of an enduring need, extending over years, is that of readying yourself for the practice of psychotherapy. While being aware of that need—excited by the idea of attainment, even taking action steps to move you toward its fulfillment—you may at various times experience the need for food, for sleep, for love, for exercise. And as each of these needs become figural within the time frame of the overriding need, you may again become aware of them, energized by them and moved to satisfy them. If you don't, they will remain unacknowledged, unexpressed and consequently unsatisfied, preventing closure and withdrawal so that the overriding need cannot be attended to. As various needs arise they must be satisfied, or satisfactorily bracketed, so that one's field may remain (at least largely) uncluttered.

Now, there has been much discussion back and forth among the faculty at the Institute as to the proper place on the cycle of "withdrawal" as opposed to "closure". Which comes before which; which follows after. "Frankly, my dears, I don't give a damn." But I do believe they're interchangeable depending on the experience. And not only interchangeable but varying over time. You may "close" a book but withdraw from it slowly, and years later some character such as "Rhett Butler" may still rear his head to haunt you. You may close the door of a house you have moved form but withdraw reluctantly form the memories it continues to convey.

In the same way one may withdraw from a love affair when one realizes that all that remains is the "ugly hope." But closure may not truly come until a new love enters the scene or another need becomes primary.

I am not as concerned with the placement of these terms as I am with the need or the resistance that is evinced in the doing of them. For example, is withdrawal a "coping" mechanism—in essence the opposite of contact—when one cannot be with another or the self, when one cannot *stand* to be there? Or is it truly part of the cycle of experience occurring after contact when the feeling tone is "I am finished; I have what I want; this is the time to stop."

Essentially there are 4 stages in the withdrawal process. The first stage emerges out of the last contact phase and is evidenced by the initial beginnings of separation. There is the re-experience of one against the other—the renewal of the sense of being separate. One is once more aware of the boundary and of the difference, the beginning of moving apart.

The second stage involves being at rest—a passive "soaking in." This may include remaining in proximity with the one just contacted (self or other). Many people short-cut this phase, attempting to account for what happened rather than allowing it to soak in.

The third stage has to do with experiencing the change that is taking place now—the sense of satisfaction that something has altered in oneself. This is a new state demanding a more active, digestive process. It involves the selection of that which will become the new me and also that which I will let go of assimilating—an internal process that some people never seem to learn, because they do not take the time to chew, digest and assimilate.

The fourth stage involves coming to rest with what has happened. There is no further need to do anything more with it. One is ready to reawaken to another piece of life.

To illustrate these stages in another way, we have:

1. Letting go—with mind *and* body
2. Reflecting
3. Affirming of what has been done
4. Ease; slower time
5. Congratulating
6. Feeling quiet
7. Feeling whole

8. Healing
9. Letting the experience settle
10. Creative space—allowing for formation of fresh figures
11. Time when what is grown in the field of our work is harvested
12. An aware non-doing place—a *being* place

As with all the points in the cycle, there are resistances to withdrawal—what Perls called the "hanging-on bite". This occurs when contact has been completed, when it is no longer nourishing but when one or the other (or both) contacting parties are loathe to let go. I recall vividly, after many years, a client I worked with who, due to her schedule, was always the last person I saw on that day. We often made good contact during the hour, but she would refuse to leave at the end of it. She would wait while I gathered up my papers, put on my coat and boots if it was snowing, walk me out to my car and stand in the parking lot talking to me through the window. Until one day I got up the gumption to put my car in gear and drive away. Ultimately we confronted the issue, but the process was painful.

The same resistance to withdrawal may accompany contact with the self or part of the self. In a sense we can become phobic about contacting the self (at least the action part of the self) because we might come to see ourselves as the only worthwhile "doer"—and so wear ourselves out rather than delegate responsibility.

It is imperative to remember that withdrawal is a natural part of the cycle of experience. It permits us to experience ourselves as o.k. and "good" in a non-doing state, and is essential to both mental and physical health and to the replenishment of the self. Without it, we remain stuck and unable to experience and satisfy a different need.

153

Closure in contrast to withdrawal appears to be fairly simple to define. It is the state of being finished. It is that point in a contact experience when there remains nothing to be added to the essence of the experience, and is characterized by a sense of completeness.

Closure is a two part process. On the one hand, one acknowledges the end of something and ties up the loose ends. On the other, one may acknowledge that something is unfinished but has to stop anyway—because of other needs which make further present contact impossible.

Closing has a style to it, a rhythm if you will. A particular individual's style may be abrupt, decisive, visible, formal and complete. Or it may be the opposite—infinite, indecisive, invisible, informal and incomplete. You might consider what style feels more like your own—which you might prefer to develop or keep.

Bear in mind that the resistance to closure is simply "not finishing", and that not finishing may go on for a long, long time.

I remember somewhat nostalgically a former client of mine who had married and was moving to Mexico. During our last session together she positioned herself as far as possible from me as she could get in my office, closed herself off in posture and communication, and sat stubbornly silent as if there was nothing left to be said. No way would I buy this. I told her how very much I would miss her, how many things I had learned from her and the manifold memories I would cherish from our time together.

At this point she dissolved into tears, saying that she was trying to make the parting less real by not referring to it or acknowledging what had been between us. She then asked if she could possibly sit on my lap while I held her and, given permission, she sat and sobbed while I stroked her hair until she was able to verbalize all the feelings, wishes and regrets that she had been withholding.

If none of this had happened she would have left—withdrawn, unable to think of me with pleasure, unable to conceive of the possibility of meeting again, but with the ghost of me haunting some of her pleasure in her new situation.

Unless one says goodbye—temporarily or permanently, there is no good way to treasure and think about the other. In this instance a closure provided the possibility for continuance. And for me—a friend in Mexico.

INTERVIEW

14
INTERVIEW WITH
GORDON WHEELER

The following interview between Gordon Wheeler and Rainette Fantz is excerpted from a recording made in Cleveland Heights, USA, in 1991.

G.W.   I'm sitting here with Rennie Fantz—Rainette
       Eden Fantz—master therapist, co-founder of the Gestalt
       Institute of Cleveland, and pioneer of psychotherapeutic
       work with dreams, metaphors, images, fantasy and play...
       I thought I would start right off with asking you: What is a
       dream?

R.F.   In Gestalt parlance, a dream is an existential message
       from the unconscious. It's a creative act—much as a
       choreographed scene, or a poem, or a drama—that the
       person has authored and that tells us about the self. A
       dream tells us what we don't always know right at the
       front of our minds or the tops of our heads.

G.W.   What is the Gestalt approach to dreams?

R.F.   The Gestalt approach to dreams deals with the
       individual—the dreamer—*playing out* all the different
       segments of the dream. The different elements—whether
       they be human or animal or furniture or something in
       nature—the individual owns these parts of the dream, tells
       the therapist (or whoever is working with her) what she

157

would be like if she *were* those parts. And one of the things we have her do is act out the different parts.

G.W. This makes me think of your background in the arts, particularly in theatre. Could you talk about how that comes into your work?

R.F. I'm a dramatic therapist, among other things. One of the ways theatre comes into my work is when I'm setting up a two-chair dialogue. The client, being one part of the self, sits in *this* chair and imagines another part of the self in *that* chair. Sometimes when an individual cannot get in touch with a particular part of the self, I become that part of the self and play it, much as I would on the stage.

G.W. So the same process can be intrapersonal or interpersonal...

R.F. Yes, you can work either way. Either they can act the whole thing out themselves—or be the whole thing themselves—or I can make it less dangerous, less threatening by taking on a part myself.

G.W. This leads in my mind to something we don't often think about in therapy, which is: What about dreams in a group?

R.F. That's fascinating. Normally when I do a group— particularly a group that is oriented around dreams—I will ask the dreamer to tell the dream, ask the whole group to hear it, then have the dreamer cast the dream using the different people in the room. Or the dreamer can direct it. Or the therapist can be the director—and fascinating things happen when one does that because not only does the *dreamer* get a sense of who he is and who he could be, but other people in the group who take on even a small part can experience themselves in a new way—can be *more* than what they normally think of themselves.

G.W. And I suppose that these parts are not randomly assigned—there's some meaning to those projections, some meaning to asking this particular person to play this particular part...

R.F. Absolutely. It depends on the dreamer: how he sees, or how she sees. Or if the people in the workshop choose their own parts in the dream, then they're picking either a part of themselves that they're not acquainted with and want to get to know, or they're acting out a part they're very familiar with. Both ways, it's very interesting and exciting.

G.W. You're speaking of workshops—an experience of yours which I've seen, and it is so dramatic and growth-ful. Let's shift to ongoing therapy. Where does this kind of work fit? How do you know when to go with a dream? Is there a good dream? A not-good dream? How does it fit into the ongoing work?

R.F. First of all, I think any dream is a good dream. The way we work them, they all have "happy endings." Sally Quinn just wrote a book called *Happy Endings*—I don't know how it is going to end (I assume happily)—but when we work the dreams, something good can always comes out of it.

Now you ask me when do I use it? Not as much as I would like. It's difficult to get people to remember their dreams. They get scared. They think , for example, that this is a nightmare and if I work it, I'm going to be in terrible shape afterwards. Or they say "I don't dream." Well, you and I know that everyone dreams. Constantly. But they don't necessarily remember their dreams. The people who refuse to remember their dreams are probably refusing to face their existence.

G.W. Say that again

R.F. People who do not remember their dreams, consistently, are probably refusing to confront their existence.

G.W. Meaning where they are in their lives, some particular issue, they are living blindly...

R.F. All that. They are working on one level, a level they have control of—or think they do—and moving in ways that

159

feel right but may not be. And are not looking at parts of themselves, parts of their environment, parts of the world that *are* their world. They are not choosing to see themselves in that world, in that part, in that piece of themselves.

G.W.   That's very colorful. You're talking about going on with the question of reluctance, or resistance, or inability to remember. How would you approach it or handle it differently at a different stage in therapy? If somebody walks in with a dream, or you've known them for a while—what about that?

R.F.   If a person walks in with a dream, and they're excited about the dream, I will immediately devote the whole hour to it.

You want to know the process?

G.W.   The process of how you would devote the hour to it? Whatever, you want to say about that, sure!

R.F.   This is how we work dreams, essentially: first, I would have the person tell me the dream and after they do that I would relate it back to them as I heard it and we'd talk about it.

This gets difficult sometimes, because dreams can be very long, and hard to remember, and it's not easy. But it gives them a chance to fill in the parts that I have left out and call out something that might be important.

G.W.   So first there's the process of contact between the two of you, some kind of empathic connection because you're not just using the same words, you've got the salient things, or they will correct you...

R.F.   They'll correct me. And after we've done that, I will enumerate all the different elements of the dream that occur to me. And then if it's a short dream we'll work through all the elements as I described earlier. But if it's a long dream, I'll ask them to pick the part that has the most energy for them.

This gets tricky because they will often pick the easiest parts, and usually something that's difficult will get neglected. So later I insist that we play one of the those parts.

For example, let's say an individual dreams of an octopus, and I try to get them to be that octopus and they say "no way, I'm not like the octopus!" Well, OK, if you're not like the octopus, tell me all the ways that you are *unlike* the octopus. And we start doing that.

G.W. So you're just as happy to heighten either pole of some internal split.

R.F. Yes, I couldn't care less. Either way they want to go, I will take them. And what they discover if they then become the things they're not, is that "By God, yes I am!"

G.W. So behind what you're saying is a great faith in an integrative tendency, an integrative capacity or need in the person that you're working with. Which would be very different than some other models of therapy.

R.F. Yes, I think so. The basic difference I always consider when I think of, for example, psychoanalysis and Freudian-type dreams, is that the Freudians regard the dream as a disguise—I think they think it's a message from the unconscious, too—but at any rate, it's hidden. They feel that what one dreams about are things that are too difficult to face. I don't believe that. I believe that they represent *all* the different parts of the self; and some parts are not so scary.

G.W. But you did speak of not facing something if you couldn't remember your dreams, and spoke of the dream as a problem to be solved—something one didn't know about oneself. So it could be difficult or hard to face.

R.F.   But if one leaves it there—rather than something that one part of the self is trying to tell another part of the self—it's a different ball of wax.

G.W.   One thing that strikes me very much—speaking of that positive, integrative, optimistic force underlying your approach—is how collaborative the work you've described so far is.

I think that many people hold a stereotype of Gestalt dream work as rather an authoritarian approach: "Do this and do that." But this whole process seems to be one of co-creating (if I may say) the *relevant* dream that you're going to work with. Which may not be the whole dream—part of which is forgotten and part of which does not stand out—but this process is very interactive and you're really partners in working this dream.

R.F.   We have to be. It is one of the reasons that I advise people starting out *not* to work dreams on their own. One of the things they're going to do is leave out that pertinent part that they don't want to face immediately and which I insist that they acquaint themselves with. And I help them. If they can't start it, for example, I may act out one role for them. This is another place where the theatre comes in.

G.W.   Why don't we shift gears for a moment. You've trained I don't know how many hundreds and thousands of students, treated hundreds and thousands of patients for the better part of four decades. And what I want to know is: how do you stay so fresh with the work? We hear so much about therapist burnout today... What energizes you—what keeps you so young and vital with this kind of work? Is it in the work itself? Is it something you draw from somewhere else?

R.F.   I think that it has to be both. People fascinate me. People have always fascinated me.

G.W. I think it's also something to do with your approach to your work—and I want to know what it is. For instance, in watching you work, it seems to me that a lot of different things are offered. You never go with the negative. I don't mean that you avoid the difficult, the conflictual, the tragic even...

R.F. I don't let it remain down. I think that's what you're saying.

G.W. If you go into it it's because you think it's coming out somewhere.

R.F. I hope, anyway.

G.W. You have an eye for the lively, the life-affirming part.

R.F. And where something *could* go, as opposed to the way people see it going consistently, which is down.

G.W. We spoke a little bit about your background in theatre, and I made some reference to your background in other arts. You often use—or seize on or make work for you—images and metaphors. Let's talk about that a little bit. What do you do with the metaphor and the fantasy when it's not a dream, but it still has that dream-like quality? How do you work with that?

R.F. Often I work with metaphor and fantasy much as if it were a dream.

For example, if I have a person fantasizing that they're going through a dark wood, I might add something in. I might say that at some point in the wood they're confronted by the entrance to a cave. I ask them to go into the cave and spend some time there, and then tell me what they see.

G.W. Is this a fantasy that they brought in?

R.F. This is a guided fantasy, but it could be either. Because I'd have taken them through that wood, past the stream and into the cave. At that point the fantasy becomes their own, it's no longer guided.

163

What they see in that cave came out of them, not out of me. So when they report back to me what they saw, I work it the same way I work a dream: I have them become the different parts of those things that they saw in the cave. And then we work it from there.

Now, metaphor is somewhat different. Metaphor bases a lot on a primary process.

G.W.   What do you mean by primary process? Are you using it in the psychodynamic, Freudian sense?

R.F.   I'm using it in the Freudian sense at this point.

G.W.   Something unguarded and spontaneous...

R.F.   It's what children do before they get to the ego function. It's the infant at the mother's breast: thinking, feeling, sensing that they can make anything happen.

G.W.   I think in the Freudian model, it's fair to say that all of that is devalued—something to get over, the primary process...

R.F.   Indeed, they want to move to the secondary process, to the ego functions. But I think we've done so much of that, that by God, it's time to get back to primary process. Get back to picturing the lovely, lovely lady in the tower.

If one is in a group, for example, and one sees a woman with long blond hair that reminds one of Rapunzel, one then thinks of her as Rapunzel. This is the metaphor for this woman. Then the need to rescue comes up in this individual. And something happens between those two people as a result of the metaphor of Rapunzel.

G.W.   How might this initially come up? Is it a chance remark? Is it something you bring in?

R.F.   Could be either. When I teach metaphor, for example, I talk and people get ideas. My sense is that this is based on our total... on all the things we've seen in the world, all the things we've read, all the history we talk about and remember, all the art the architecture. All of these go into metaphor. And if I ask people to allow themselves to think in that fashion, they can do it!

There are some marvelous games we play in workshops where I ask one person to go out of the room and then those of us in the room pick one person that we are going to make "it"—the person that we are going to make metaphors about. When the person comes back into the room, they ask questions of the whole group to find out who is "it." "What kind of book is this person?" "What kind of music?" "What kind of fictional character?" Whatever.

And we in the group, including the person who's "it," answer metaphorically.

G.W.   Once again what is standing out for me is the way you're always looking for an expansion of self. Once you've got these 12 or 20 metaphors about this person, they've got a lot of stuff to take up some relationship to. I don't know whether they'll lay it out, project it, but something has to happen.

R.F.   One of the things that happens is that if the metaphors fit the person who is being described, we let it go. If they don't understand where it comes from, if they don't own them, if it doesn't feel right to them, then they can ask "What about me made you think of this particular metaphor?"

And then when the other group member describes all those things, the person can say "Ah yes, I can see where that comes from," or "I can't, and I'll fight it to the death."

G.W.   But to fight it is to enter into a more vibrant relationship with a (potentially) new part of the self.

R.F.   Absolutely.

G.W.   Speaking of the enlargement of the self, and the fertility, and the different parts you can go into... What's in there?

What sources speak to you? What writers, what dramatists—since you've been an actress—or what poets? You often make references to poetry or quote bits from poems.

R.F.   I remember quoting one to you yesterday.

G.W.   Yes, you quoted Browning.

R.F.   I did, I did. "Let your reach exceed your grasp, or what's a Heaven for?" I own that one.

I believe it, and I have always tried to reach a little further than I've done before—and God knows I've done a lot of things. (*Laughter*)

G.W.   (*Laughter*) But you haven't run out of new ones.

R.F.   I'm not sure. We'll find out.

G.W.   Are there other writers that come to your mind, now or in the past? In childhood?

R.F.   Speaking of childhood—*Winnie the Pooh*! Not only did I love it then, but I love it with my daughter. One read it any number of times, Christopher Robin... *Charlotte's Web*—a marvelous, marvelous... I just adore EB White. Which reminds me of *The Once and Future King*—another of my favorites.

G.W.   King Arthur—the sword and the stone.

R.F.   Yes. Various points of view. Originally from the male point of view, and then more later when the feminists moved in and started writing.

G.W.   There's a new book out, a great big novel—you probably know more about it than I do—the retelling of the Arthurian myths and legends, but from a woman's point of view: *Mysts of Avalon*.

R.F.   I read the *Mysts of Avalon*—and that came out a number of years ago. There was that one, and there was another one that...

G.W.   When you first said Arthur, I thought you might cast yourself as Merlin, but...

R.F.   That's my cat.

G.W.   ...now that you're...

R.F.   I don't know. There are parts of me that are Morgan Le Fey, but I am not in total Morgan Le Fey. She is probably wickeder than I am at my wickedest.

G.W.   I don't know the character that well, and I don't know if I know how wicked you are at your wickedest.

R.F.   Well, you probably don't! Anyway, those are some of them. I grew up in a house that had a large library of the classics, so I grew up with Walter Scott, Jane Austen, Mark Twain...

G.W.   I could've made that relationship because you have a penchant for the trenchant remark that I associate with Jane Austen.

R.F.   Yes! Those are the books I read growing up. I read voraciously—all the time. I have read many many many many mysteries, which I love... I read novels. I think novels are exciting.

G.W.   Ones that are in your apperceptive mass, that you like to quote from. What about poets? You were quoting from...

R.F.   ...Browning... Shakespeare, of course, is there.

G.W.   Great parts for women. Did you ever play any of them?

R.F.   Ah-hah. Lady MacBeth.

G.W.   Ah! *(Laughter)*

R.F.   *(Laughter)*...At my wickedest!.... Then I was thinking of his sonnets, which are so lovely. Reminds me of E.B. Browning; "How do I love thee?" But I think of Shakespeare's sonnets as so very different. "My love is not a red red rose"... Or no—"My love is not a summer's day, she is more..."

G.W.   "...Beautiful and more temperate..."

R.F.   Yes. "Temperate." He's written so many fantastic things...

And the Russian writers are exciting. Chekhov's plays of course—in which I played several parts...

G.W.   What have you played?

R.F.   I played in *Uncle Vanya*. I did Yeliena, who was essentially the leading lady in the show, but not the best part. The best part's Sonia, the young girl. The niece.

G.W.   I don't know the play. I know *The Cherry Orchard*, the stories, but not that play.

R.F.   It's a great show. And it was a very exciting show to do, because there were two characters in there that I played against: the one I was married to, and the one I was in love with. And there was a fight between my husband and me which just absolutely *caught fire*, because the two of us played off each other—and *that* was exciting...

Anyway, there's *The Brothers Karamazov*, there's... Oh my, there's so many books. So many books.

G.W.   Go back to the question of the witch. Morgan Le Fay.

R.F.   (*Laughter*) Oh, right!

G.W.   You do deal in your work with transforming people...

R.F.   That's so.

G.W.   ...Or creating some conditions where that happens.

R.F.   I do not transform them, but as you say...

G.W.   It *has* been said that you cast a spell.

R.F.   That has been said, yes.

G.W.   What is the transformation in psychotherapy? What's the goal of psychotherapy? What's the point?

R.F.   In my way of looking at it, it's about finding the *complete whole* as opposed to the fragmented parts. That the individual can *own* all of—and here we go back to the dreams, but it's the same thing in psychotherapy—that the individual can own all of the disowned parts of the self. They can re-own the old parts, and they can *expand* the

168

self. They become *more* than they were when they came in.

G.W.   So it's a creative process...

R.F.   Yes...

G.W.   ...A *growing* that you are—midwifing?

R.F.   Hopefully.

G.W.   Facilitating? Provoking?

R.F.   All of those things, yes.

G.W.   Do you consider the person you're working with a patient or a client or an artist?

R.F.   Hopefully by the end of therapy he's an artist. Often at the beginning of therapy he may be an artist, but he's an artist with his hands tied behind him. He can't do the sculpture or the painting...

G.W.   So his medium at that point is symptoms, if you will... Or hers...

R.F.   Or hers...

G.W.   And what *is* the person that artists are?

R.F.   The self.

G.W.   So it all comes back to the self.

R.F.   It all comes back to the self. How much can there be of me? How much of me can I use—how much can I accept. I have to accept it before I can use it. It doesn't matter how much is hidden in there, if it cannot be accessed and if it cannot be put into working.

G.W.   So first thing is to come into some relationship with it that will lead toward owning it. And then this integration that we keep referring to happens and the person has a larger self to go out from.

R.F.   Yes.

G.W.   How wonderful.

R.F.   It is! It's exciting. So exciting.

G.W.   Let's talk about how you—as an artist, an actress—as a young woman—got into psychology and got involved with the Gestalt school...

R.F.   Well, it was accidental. I happened to be married to a psychiatrist, and at the same time that I was doing commercial art and getting bored with it, I thought it might be useful to take a few courses at Case Western Reserve so that I could talk to my husband about his own field.

Well I don't know if it made it easier to talk to him, but it certainly got me involved because I then changed my major. I only expected to take a few courses and quit, but I finished my undergraduate work in psychology and went into graduate work in psychology. That was about the time that Bill Barkley went to New York to attend a Fritz Perls workshop...

G.W.   Ah—that was when the Gestalt model was first being articulated in the early 50's by Goodman and Perls.

R.F.   Yes, exactly. At that time, Bill Barkley was partner with my husband, Jeff. So when he came back and decided that we absolutely had to have Perls here, he invited me (as a real novice; I wasn't doing anything in the field yet except studying) to be a part of that original group.

So that's how I got involved with that Perlsian stuff.

G.W.   And you've become one of the shapers and creators of the whole field...

R.F.   If not one of the movers... (*Laughter*)

G.W.   That, too! (*Laughter*)

How has your work changed over time? Particularly, how has your work with dreams changed over time? You certainly work in a way that is very different than the way that Perls worked, although it may seem similar...

R.F.   Only the beginnings are similar. Perls was the one who wanted people to become the different parts of the dream, so they could connect with them. But he never worked the dreams the way we now work them. It was that people *needed* to be those things, he felt. To *be* them. Then they could just get with it, and he didn't have to do a damn thing, you see? Whereas I take it much further than that. Once the person has become the different parts, I will talk to the different parts, play out the polarities, do them in groups...

G.W.   Or dialogue with them yourself...

R.F.   As you know from our work together, we get far afield and go into whatever the dream evokes, so that if one is being the mother of an element in the dream, we may switch to having that individual actually have a conversation with her real mother—and play both parts. Now it's no longer a clear-cut polarity, but it's working in a way that is therapeutic, not simply "dream work." Not that dream work isn't therapeutic, but it's leading...

G.W.   But it grew out of that... Speaking of working together, I remember a dream I had that you worked with me years ago—that we have on tape and use illustrative excerpts from. This was years ago now. It strikes me, viewing that tape, how *young* we both were.

R.F.   Well, we were, Gordon.

G.W.   We were, I guess, at the time. I still think that it's an excellent illustration of how you work—how different and how much more free it is from the original process. What I remember is dreaming of unburied bodies in the basement...

R.F.   I remember...

G,W.   And using your view of embodied metaphor: going with the metaphor of the dream, you asked me what was unburied in my life. Which goes back to your original statement that the dream is an existential message, and also your statement about people who aren't facing their lives—aren't facing something in their lives.

171

R.F.   As you say that now, I think I could have just as easily
        said "How do you deaden yourself? Same idea. Which
        Fritz would *never* have done.

G.W.   I didn't know Fritz, but I can see him saying that.

R.F.   Well, he wouldn't have done it with dreams, because he
        didn't do the work part of the dreams.

G.W.   How has your work changed over the years?

R.F.   My dream work or my general psychotherapy?

G.W.   Both.

R.F.   I think they've both become looser, in a sense. When I
        first started working with dreams, I think I stayed very
        close to the laid-out pattern. Anyway, I don't know....
        I'm who I am now, and how I work is a reflection of how
        I've changed... But I'm not sure how I've changed.

G.W.   Anything about it come to you?

R.F.   I can be tougher, I think. Which is good. I was always
        so... helpful, so supportive—that was a big part of me. I
        have become more confrontative. And sometimes less
        so, which goes together... it works out fine, because it
        still has a happy ending.

G.W.   What's a happy ending?

R.F.   A happy ending is finally owning a part of the dream and
        thinking "My God, I can use this, I know that I can use
        this, I know it will work." That's a happy ending.

G.W.   What do you have to say to the young person starting out
        as a psychotherapist, or the older person starting out...

R.F.   (Sigh.) Oh yes... Don't play the role of psychotherapist.
        For the love of God, be who you are. Be immediate.
        Don't sit back and let the client see you as a blank screen.
        Reveal what you are feeling.

G.W.   Why? Because this is a crucial difference in schools...

R.F.   One reason is that the therapist is a model for the client.
        And if the therapist makes a nothing of themselves, the

172

client will always feel that they can't be spontaneous, that they can't be where they are, that they have to wear a mask. And I think that psychotherapy is a process of removing masks, rather than putting them on.

G.W. You're looking for the authentic self.

R.F. I am.

G.W. And you're confronted with the false self.

R.F. Um-hmm. Well, the limited self. It's not necessarily false, but it is masked. The person who comes to therapy is often scared. They're scared of change and they know they need to change.

When I'm in my study, I have these huge black chairs, and one would normally sit facing the client. I don't sit like that. I sit with my feet over the arms of the chair, or up under me, or whatever. And I see very gradually how my clients shift their position from being stiff and hidden to being easy and comfortable. You see?

That's one of the things that I do, that I *never* would have done when I started therapy.

They're the same chairs (*laughter*). I've had those chairs for 30 years.

G.W. And what about the psychotherapist—Gestalt or otherwise—who doesn't use dreams?

R.F. I'll tell them, "You know, you can get along without dreams—I get along without dreams often—but you're limiting your own material."

G.W. What are you missing?

R.F. You're not using a tool that can immediately get your client or patient—whatever you want to call him— into a different part of himself.

G.W. You always go to that different part.

R.F. Because I do not want him to let himself off. I want him to face the good and beautiful and ugly and evil—and

173

know when it's appropriate to use all or any of them. And know when it isn't appropriate.

G.W. It's inspiring. And what about the therapist who works with dreams, but from another theoretical perspective? What would you say out of the Gestalt perspective? Is there message you'd like to give to that person?

R.F. It's the message I've been giving all along... That so many of the other methods of working with dreams do not get the dreamer to identify with other parts of the self—or even the parts they recognize. They don't get them to recognize the holes, the emptinesses, the lacunae that are in the dream.

G.W. So you also work with what's not in the dream.

R.F. I very much work with what's not in the dream.

G.W. Can you say more about that?

R.F. Yes! Because that's intriguing. Say that a person dreams of a Southern plantation house with these marvelous balconies. But there are no pillars supporting these balconies. That's a hole, an emptiness. What they have is a lack of support. Just moving from the lack of a supporting pillar in the dream, one can move to a lack of support in the self—and then try to discover how one can build those supports, regain them, find them outside oneself.

G.W. Again I see a metaphorical leap that you bring to it, for the patient to validate or not.

R.F. We always need their validation...

G.W. It's a co-creation.

R.F. Certainly. We cannot force a metaphor of value onto a client.

G.W. So what about the interpretation of dreams? *The Interpretation of Dreams* is almost the seminal work in the field of psychotherapy. What is interpretation in your view? Does it have a role in Gestalt work?

174

R.F.   Well, minorly. When I think of Freud, I think that he sees each symbol as always meaning the same thing. Snake is a penis is a penis is a penis. A vase is a womb, a vagina, whatever. It doesn't change! Whereas in Gestalt therapy, dream therapy, the person can make anything at all out of a symbol. Again, *they* are the artist.

G.W.   So who creates the new understanding which is the interpretation? The patient? The therapist? The two of you together?

R.F.   It's the two of us together, although ultimately it's the patient. And you know, if they find some difficulty in getting to a particular part, I can say, "You know if that were me, if I were that particular part, this is how I would see myself. But you are someone totally different than me, and I don't know if this means anything to you. If it does, hey, take it! If it doesn't, we'll toss it aside, we always have a wastebasket handy."

G.W.   What do you still want to do in your work that you haven't done yet, what grabs you?

R.F.   Mmmmm, Gordon!

G.W.   I'm again thinking of the freshness piece, because you are so inspiring and alive with this work. What's the ongoing edge?

R.F.   I don't know. I think that I discover it as it happens. I don't think that I can predict it. Where I am today I may be tomorrow, but I may not. Something new may occur in a therapy session that takes me down another path that I have never used before.

G.W.   You make me feel that if I could give up planning, I could remain as young as you have!

R.F.   I don't recommend it to you necessarily, because your planning results in such marvelous things. It resulted in a magnificent new theoretical approach to Gestalt.

G.W.   Thank you, I don't know if that was the result of planning or one of the dead parts of my life that you were referring to...

R.F.   You must have planned to sit down and write. And whether or not you knew what you were going to write about is something else. When I sit down to write, it happens as I write. I don't know precisely what I'm going to say, but as I write, ideas come. So maybe I'll do some more writing, Gordon, or maybe I won't.

G.W.   I hope you will. Some of the things we have talked about today...

R.F.   It's more fun doing it this way.

G.W.   Yes, it is!

IN MEMORY OF RENNIE:
A PERSONAL EPILOGUE

"Nothing Lasts forever. In this world, there is a kind of
painful progress. Longing for what we've left behind, and
dreaming ahead... At least I think that's so..."
—Tony Kushner, *Angels in America,*
Part Two: Perestroika

I am honored indeed to be writing this epilogue to *The Dreamer and the Dream*, the collected writings of Rainette Eden Fantz—healer, magician, mentor, friend. Writing of "Rennie," as she was known to students, patients, colleagues and friends alike (and many had been all four, at one time or another) brings her presence back to me now, the vivid embodiment that was Rennie's color, energy and form. This presence itself was a paradox, a union of polarities encompassing illness and transcendence, fragility and vitality, sensuality and formlessness, magic and helplessness in the face of a harsh reality. Most of all, to me Rennie stood for a kind of celebration—of life, of style, of *self*, in the best sense of that overworked term: your self, her own self, the expansion and relation of one self to another in new creative forms. Today, with all the current attention paid, in Gestalt and in psychotherapy at large, to the issue of shame, I think of Rennie as loving life shamelessly, in many dimensions that are a challenge for most of us to live fully and without inhibition. She was shameless about performing and starring; shameless about her femaleness and sexuality; shameless of her own beauty and enjoyment of acknowledgement and appreciation; and finally, shameless about the debility and ultimately the deformity of her body in illness and decline, the long minutes it took her to enter a room and get in and out of a chair, to eat, to do any little task that the rest of us take for granted.

A poem written by Rennie's friend and fellow faculty member at GIC, Jody Telfair, captures the image that holds me now:

> Enchanted
> They listen as she hums her stories
> Of Love and Sorrow,
> Pain and Romance.
> As autumn arrives
> Her lovely misshapen branches
> Droop graciously
> Heavy with fruit for greedy hands,
> And full with color
> Red amber gold
> For hungry hearts.
> Softening with an ancient
> Wistful smile
> She smiles and endures.

To her cohort of founding teachers at the Gestalt Institute of Cleveland, as to the generation of teachers after, Rennie was an inspiration. Here are the words of her colleague Elaine Kepner, whose own career has taken her around the country and the world in the public field of organizational behavior and development, which she helped to found—the kind of wider prominence that illness denied to Rennie in the second half of her life:

> To me you were colleague, friend, artist, teacher, scholar, writer, psychologist, playmate, Mother, Wife. As a Gestalt therapist you gained international recognition as the Grand Doyenne of metaphor, language, fantasies, and dreams—those realms of communication which both reflect and transform our experiencing. You knew the secrets of transforming the unfamiliar into a form of enlightenment. I cherish the

memories of watching your outbursts of enthusiasm
when someone you were working with grabbed the
tiger by the tail.... In community with each other, we
tell our stories to enfold you in our hearts once again.

In Rennie all the Woman archetypes were at play at once:
Coquette, Sister, Lover, Dancer, Earth Mother, Queen, Witch,
Crone—and finally the Wounded Healer, who draws from her
own wound the magic elixir of a healing potion for others. She
celebrated the best that life could offer, but brought no shrinking
or false sentiment to the limitations and shadow aspects of
others—or of herself. For her own strength and courage she drew
in turn on those she fed and healed, reveling in the social energy
of the group, and then in the intimacy she created with special
others. Most of all she reveled in and drew vitality from her
beloved daughter, Lorian Fantz, herself a gifted artist like her
mother. In Lori she saw not herself again, but a new being, a late
blessing in a midlife already shadowed with illness, an endless
marvel of new talents and joys. When grandchildren came, their
pictures joined Lori's in Rennie's handbag, and their names joined
their mother's on her mother's lips.

The story of Rennie's passing is as remarkable as her life
itself. The time was February, 1994. The faculty of the Gestalt
Institute of Cleveland, which Rennie had helped to found and
which had been her home community and second family for so
long, were gathered for their annual retreat. Rennie's absence was
on everyone's mind—it was the first such gathering she had
missed in forty years. Indeed, racked with the combined effects of
decades of illness and decades of treatment, some of it as
debilitating as the illness itself, Rennie had not been expected to
hold out all through the past month. But she *had* held out, as if
waiting for her friends and beloved community to be gathered
together one more time. Now she lay in a coma in a nearby
hospital, on life supports, past the reach of medicine's healing and
damage alike.

It was a time of generational transition for the Institute. As part of this process, the faculty were joined by the well-known ceremonial artist Cynthia Gale. In an earth ritual, Cynthia had invited each faculty member present to select a simple gray stone from a basket she had brought, and write on it a single wish, thought, or intention for the community. When all the stones had been placed back in the basket, each of us was to pick one again and read it: thus each intention would come to belong to and be spoken by the whole community. Gordon Wheeler, who after that gathering was on his way to sit through the night at Rennie's deathbed vigil, asked if he might be the last to select a stone, and take the last one remaining to Rennie. The group agreed, and all the stones were read out in turn, with all their words of vision and intentionality for the Institute and our community: richness, learning, healing for ourselves and others, new creative spirit, honoring of self and other, and so forth. When Gordon selected the last stone from the basket and read it out loud, it simply said: "Rennie is going home."

The group sat stunned at the synchronicity, one of those moments where the power of the transpersonal is simply as real and as tangible as earth, air, fire and water. To his amazement, when Gordon arrived at Rennie's hospital room a short while later, he found her alert and awake from her coma, weakened but completely herself. When I arrived somewhat after that, I walked in on the two of them singing show tunes. "Getting to Know You," is one I think of now from that night. And, with aching poignancy, "Whistle a Happy Tune"—"Make believe you're brave, and you'll soon believe you are," they warbled together. "You can be as brave—as you make believe you are."

Rennie was brave. Her courage and her indomitable will were on every lip at her memorial some days later. It wasn't pretending with her—it was the power of imagination, and the inspiration of the company of her loved ones that sustained her always. In retrospect now, I find myself wondering if her illness didn't require of her a sort of suspension of ordinary reality, that heightened capacity for metaphor and fantasy, dream and drama that marked her work and made her the superb and unique clinician she was. Life has a way of burying the richest treasures in the most unexpected places. To celebrate Rennie is to celebrate life in all its wonder, its twistings like her tortured hands, its secrets and its mystery.

For me, writing these lines has been another leavetaking. To Rennie, I say thank you, and goodbye once more. To the reader, I invite you to let this contact with a rare spirit renew your commitment to a competency that always has room for awe and wonder, and an enthusiasm for living that renews and refreshes itself in the marvel of each new moment, which always brings a new dream image, a new mystery, and a new creative possibility.

Dorothy Siminovitch
Cleveland, Ohio
Spring, 1998

REFERENCES

Bandler, R & Grinder, J. (1975). *The Structure of Magic*. Palo Alto: Science and Behavior Books, Inc.

Green, Hannah. (1964). *I Never Promised You a Rose Garden*. New York: Henry Holt & Co.

Highet, Gilbert. (1945). *Man's Unconquerable Mind*. New York: Columbia University Press.

Jaynes, Julian. (1976). *The Origin of Consciousness in the Breakdown of the Bicameral Mind*. Boston: Houghton Mifflin Company.

Perls, Frederick. (1965). Gestalt Therapy and Human Potentialities. Esalen Paper No.1, June, 1965

Reich, Wilhelm. (1949). *Character Analysis*. New York: Orgone Institute Press

Reinhardt, Max. (1949). The enchanted sense of play. In Cole, T. & Chinoy, H.K. (Eds.), *Actors on Acting*. New York: Crown Publishers, Inc.

Sonenberg, J. (with Roberts, A.). (In Press). *Threshold of the Unconscious*.

Stoehr, Taylor. Personal communication

Wheeler, Gordon. (1991). *Gestalt Reconsidered*. New York: Gardner Press.

ABOUT THE AUTHOR

RAINETTE EDEN FANTZ, PH.D., was active as a professional actor until debilitating arthritis caused her to switch careers in her mid-thirties. She received her doctorate from Western Reserve University in Cleveland, and went on to study Gestalt therapy with Fritz & Laura Perls, Paul Goodman, Isadore From and others. She was a founding member of the Gestalt Institute of Cleveland, and director of its post-graduate intensive training program. Renowned for her work with dreams, metaphor and fantasy, she was a beloved teacher in the Cleveland area for over thirty years. As a core member of the GIC faculty, Dr. Fantz was instrumental in developing a new school of psychotherapy, and taught thousands of professionals from around the world.

ABOUT THE EDITOR

ARTHUR ROBERTS, MA, received his undergraduate degree from The Massachusetts Institute of Technology and his Masters from Lesley College Graduate School. Originally educated in the physical sciences, he later trained as an actor with Alan Brody, Janet Sonenberg, Terry Schreiber and Uta Hagen. He maintains a private practice of psychotherapy and teaches psychology in the Boston area, where he is also active in theatre as an actor and as a consultant to the Music & Theater Arts Department at M.I.T. His work has been published internationally in scientific journals, psychotherapy periodicals, books, and literary magazines.

Please address book-related correspondence to the editor. He may be contacted via post at 250 Commonwealth Ave., Boston MA 02116; or via the internet at "aroberts@alum.mit.edu"